Embodying Hope

Also by Sonia Connolly

Wellspring of Compassion: Self-Care for Sensitive People Healing from Trauma

Presence After Trauma: Reconcile with Your Self and the World

Embodying Hope

Living in Difficult Times with a Difficult Past

Sonia Connolly

Sundown Healing Arts
Portland, Oregon

Copyright © 2021 by Sonia Connolly
All rights reserved. No part of this book may be reproduced in any form by any electronic or mechanical means including photocopying, recording, or information storage and retrieval without permission in writing.
Published by Sundown Healing Arts, Portland, Oregon
SundownHealingArts.com
Requests for permission to make copies of any part of the work can be submitted to orders@sundownhealingarts.com.
For bulk orders, write to orders@sundownhealingarts.com.
File under: SELF-HELP/Post-Traumatic Stress Disorder (PTSD)
Printed in the United States of America

Cover Graphic Design: Luna Enriquez
Cover photo: Robert Bye on Unsplash
Desert Boulders, Ein Gedi, Israel
Chapter heading illustrations: Robyn Posin
Illustration credits on page 251

Library of Congress Control Number: 2020924516
ISBN-13: 978-0-9839038-4-0

FIRST EDITION

This publication is not intended as a substitute for the advice of health care professionals. Internet addresses were accessible at the time this book went to press. Content of referenced websites is solely that of their sponsors and does not necessarily reflect the opinions of the author of this book.

Client stories are fictionalized composites of common patterns seen in sessions.

Thanks to each of you for addressing these difficult times with grace and care, despite and because of past trauma.

Acknowledgments

Thanks to Robyn Posin for gently persistent encouragement at each step of this book's creation, for helpful comments on a draft, and for sharing her delightful art.

Thanks to Andy Anady for copy editing, conversations, and their expertise on gender and social justice, which made this a better book.

Thanks to all the clients who courageously shared their process with me in session.

Thanks to all the people who wrote to tell me how an article touched them.

Thanks to Ann Weiser Cornell and Barbara McGavin for the tools I have learned from their work: Inner Relationship Focusing, Treasure Maps to the Soul, and Untangling®. More information at FocusingResources.com.

Contents

Introduction: Here We Are — 1

1: Wider Narratives — 5
    Prefer Narratives with Hope — 7
    Consider Additional Truths — 11
    Offer a Collaborative Story — 15
    Practice Kind Language — 19
    Relieve Pressure: Replace Should With Could — 23
    Good Enough for Mistakes — 27
    Loosen Inner Deadlock — 31
    Resources — 35

2: Difficult Times — 37
    Withstand Ongoing Trauma — 39
    Agency in a Time of Pandemic — 43
    Adapt to New Risks — 47
    Wear a Mask to Belong — 52
    Rock the Boat About Racism — 56
    How to Resist Enough — 61
    Mend What You Can Reach — 66
    Resources — 70

3: Uncomfortable Emotions — 71
    Counter the Feelings Police — 73
    Depression: Natural Response to Trauma — 77
    Anchor Terror in Time — 82
    Lift the Anger Lid With Care — 86
    Sit with Disappointment — 91

    Make Room for Grief _____ 95
    Resonate with Loneliness _____ 99
    Resources _____ 104

4: Full Self _____ **105**
    In Search of Self-Confidence _____ 106
    Cherish Your Limits _____ 110
    The Perils of Nice _____ 113
    Balance for Your Inner Guardian _____ 117
    Healthy Entitlement: Discern Your Domain _____ 122
    Your Body is Your Ally _____ 127
    Embody Hunger, Embody Fullness _____ 132
    Resources _____ 137

5: Intricate Body _____ **139**
    The Push/Pull of Touch _____ 140
    Find Calm: Practice Rest and Regulation _____ 145
    Find Calm: A Polyvagal Primer _____ 150
    Get to Know Your Guts _____ 155
    Self-Care for Sticky Lungs _____ 160
    Let Go for More Sound _____ 165
    Look into the Present _____ 169
    Resources _____ 173

6: Relationship Skills _____ **175**
    Intervene for a Better World _____ 176
    Kindness, Not Contempt _____ 180
    Seek Nourishing Feedback _____ 184
    Careful Conflict _____ 189
    Grow Away from Enmeshment _____ 193
    The Right Distance from Family _____ 198

Support a Friend in Crisis	203
Resources	207

7: Healing Support — 209

Celebrate Small Steps	210
Solid Support for Change	213
Add Ease to Anniversaries	216
Elements of Refuge	220
When Help Means Danger	224
When Help Means Rescue	229
How to Leave Your Practitioner	234
Resources	238

Afterword: Thank You — 239

Glossary — 243

About the Author — 249

Introduction: Here We Are

You did all this personal healing work so you could have a happier life, and now look! We have ongoing white supremacy and climate change, manifesting as destructive leaders, militarized police, escalating wildfires, and a world-wide pandemic. We live in difficult times.

Many people's first line of defense is denial, shading into victim-blaming. "It's not real. I'll be fine. It won't affect me. If someone over there is getting hurt, it's because they're doing something wrong." We can move toward acceptance, compassion, collaboration, and action.

Experienced survivors. People who have gone through trauma and healing are familiar with the initial shock, disbelief, and disorientation of sudden change. We can keep functioning when a pandemic changes everything.

We have developed tolerance for terror and uncertainty. We know how to reach out for support and how to keep ourselves company when support is not available. While we can adapt to increasing stress up to a point, we also have limits and disabilities that continue to need care.

Re-embodiment. Trauma divides us from our bodies. Our survival tools of denial, dissociation, and freeze save us during terrible events, and at the same time rob us of feeling alive and connected with others.

Healing from trauma is re-embodiment, reclaiming our full present experience from those survival tools. We claim our emotional and physical pain as well as our joy and ease of movement. We sense what we want and need, as well as what we do not want and need to escape.

Benefits. As risky as it may seem after trauma, embodiment is physically safer. When we inhabit our bodies, we navigate smoothly around obstacles rather than bumping into corners and doorways. We notice subtle internal and external signals that help us take good care of ourselves.

Embodied, we can play and create. When we feel ourselves as part of the planet, we act with care for those around us.

People who are already fully themselves do not need to buy the latest marketed product to cover their shame or feelings of emptiness. People who acknowledge uncomfortable truths are less vulnerable to gaslighting. People who allow their feelings to flow can have empathy for others, and can no longer ignore the suffering caused by white supremacy.

Not knowing. While being embodied anchors us in the present, it does not help us know or control the future. Some people thrive on chaos and uncertainty, and some want stability and solid ground under their feet.

Not knowing can be used to dissociate and disengage. "I don't need to know about voter suppression efforts." It can be a painful suspension of safety. "Will that court decision take away my rights?" It can be an opening to learn more about the world and ourselves. "I don't know how to be anti-racist and I want to learn."

Hope is continuing to take action in the face of not knowing. Hope is separate from belief or faith or trust or certainty that it will all work out.

Hope accepts what we do know, sense, and feel. Knowing can be tentative, our best effort to sort through conflicting and unreliable information. We might wish things were different, but hope does not pretend them away.

For trauma survivors, hope can feel like a mockery of painful lived experience. It might feel like hope for a good outcome invites more punishment instead. The kind of hope that requires cheerful sunshine and flowers is not a good fit for stormy times.

We embody hope when we keep moving forward, one stubborn step after another, like walking through steady rain. We also embody hope when we take shelter for protection and rest. Breath is hope. The spark of life that keeps looking for a way to live in the midst of suicidal despair, that is hope. Can you sense the force of hope in your body in this moment?

Hope might feel like one of those relighting candles whose flame pops up no matter how many times it is extinguished. It might feel like gritted teeth, never letting go. It might feel like a reliable smooth stone. It might feel airy, light, confident. It might trickle through you like water from an inexhaustible spring.

Take your time. You can read this book as a continuous whole, or dip in and out, focusing on the topics that are most alive for you right now. If you feel anxious, impatient, or bored, take a break or skip the parts that feel difficult.

As you read, listen to your body and notice what is true for you with kind awareness. Tune in to your experience when you have an uninterrupted block of time to yourself, or in bits and pieces as you go about your day, whenever you have time to think and feel. Invite in comfort and support.

Robyn Posin's expressive drawing of a reclining figure at the beginning of each article reminds you, as she often says, that rest is a sacred act. She has also given kind permission to use her joyfully embodied figures at the beginning of each chapter.

The cover photo is Ein Gedi, an oasis in Israel near the Dead Sea. Reliable flowing water brings hope, relief, and abundant life to those dusty dry hills under the hot sun. I hope this book offers you respite and replenishment in these hard times.

Overview. Articles are grouped into seven themes.
1. **Wider Narratives.** Choose stories with room for new possibilities.
2. **Difficult Times.** Name what is happening, find support, and take positive action.
3. **Uncomfortable Emotions.** Turn toward your powerful emotions with compassion.
4. **Full Self.** Embrace the complexity of all of you.
5. **Intricate Body.** Delve into the details of being a body.
6. **Relationship Skills.** Relate to people around you with presence and care.
7. **Healing Support.** You are the expert on what you need to make it through.

Check the **Glossary** for definitions of unfamiliar terms.

All the links in this book are clickable at:
https://traumahealed.com/embodying-hope-links/

1: Wider Narratives

When difficult times remind us of a difficult past, we might freeze with the belief that nothing will ever change, or collapse under overwhelming change and uncertainty.

A narrative is a story we tell ourselves about how we got here, what is happening now, and what is possible in the future. Some narratives limit possibilities: "I always get hurt," or "I deserve the bad things that happen to me." Others open up possibilities and hope: "I can learn new skills."

Our default narratives are shaped by our privilege, experiences, resources, and current environment. Privilege is the set of advantages and benefits society gives us for being one or more of cisgender, straight, white, male, Christian, able-bodied, wealthy, etc. People with privilege are perceived as normal and trustworthy by default.

When we feel frozen or overwhelmed, we can look for narratives that give us more options. What is possible can change in ways that were previously unimaginable, like everyone suddenly sheltering in place from a new virus. When unexpected crises arise, unexpected help can also arise. "I give thanks for help unknown already on the way."*

We can practice stretching our narratives in different directions to gain more flexibility over time. What is a good outcome for that difficult situation and how would that feel in your body? What could that person say to repair an injured relationship? When we imagine good outcomes, we give ourselves breathing room and create new pathways in our bodies.

Give yourself credit for trying your best with the resources you have. Look for ways to improve the situations around you. Stand in your story as it is right now, and listen generously to others' stories. Stay open to new information and interpretations, without abandoning your truth.

Language is a crucial building block of narrative. We are each working to unlearn oppression and add kindness in our language and behavior. How can your narratives include understanding and respect for broader perspectives around race, gender, sexual orientation, disability and more?

As we learn and grow, we all make mistakes despite our best efforts, and we all deserve compassion and opportunities for repair. As we look back on mistakes, they often change into turning points that add new choices to our lives.

When we feel stuck about a decision or situation, stepping back and listening deeply to each part of us can help us reach an inclusive solution that was not part of the initial narrative.

When your narratives dead-end into despair, keep looking for wider narratives that open even a tiny pathway into hope.

---

* Author unknown, often credited as "Native American saying."

1: Wider Narratives

Prefer Narratives with Hope

When Naomi Ceder was young, the narrative she saw about trans people was one of sickness, wrongness, and absence of hope.* The only way to transition was to renounce contact with all family and community. There was no way forward.

Over time, she found trans people who had an affirming narrative that included staying in contact with family and community. Now she had viable options and could move forward with a more gradual, connected gender transition. Our narrative about a situation controls the options we have.

Name the problem. When you have an intractable problem, look at the narrative around it. Analogies, metaphors, and narratives define the solutions we can imagine.

You might not have a narrative at all, just a nameless, amorphous unease. Being gay or trans can feel that way if available narratives only include cis straight people. An abuse survivor might feel that way before memories surface.

If you have a problem with no narrative, hold the question of what it might be. Sit with the unease, and with what you do know about the problem. Keep an eye out for clues. Find safe people to talk with who might help you name the issue. Once you have a name, you can explore further with internet searches and people who know about that topic.

It's not you. Often, an intractable problem includes the

---

* "It's not you, it's them: Reflections on being marginalized in STEM" by Naomi Ceder at Write/Speak/Code 2016. https://vimeo.com/176695137

narrative that there is something fundamentally wrong with you, that instead of having a problem, you are the problem. This narrative and its shame might be invisible, like the air you breathe.

The first step is to notice a toxic narrative. You might arrive there through despair. When you have tried everything to fix yourself, exhausted defeat leads you to put down the shovel of self-blame and stop digging. You might arrive there by paying attention to beliefs that make you feel terrible, and deciding to choose new beliefs.

It can feel misleadingly powerful to label yourself as the problem and try to fix it. Unfortunately, you cannot fix what is not broken. When you name that the problem is external to you, you might feel helpless and overwhelmed. You might also feel relief, because you have shifted to being on your own side rather than attacking yourself.

You are not alone. When your narrative says that you are the problem, it also says that you are solely responsible for it, and maybe you should not even talk about it. When the narrative shifts to an external problem, it shifts from individual to universal. You have company and support, because many people are affected by the same external environment.

Being trans is intrinsic to the person, and not bad. The problem lies not in being trans, but in how society treats trans people. We can all work together to reduce anti-trans bigotry and improve resources for trans people. Trans people can share hopeful narratives of exploring gender expression and finding a good fit. For some, that includes the relief of taking hormones that feel congruent with their bodies.

Being abused is bad, and not intrinsic to the person. The problem lies not in being an abuse survivor, but in how society treats abuse survivors, and in the internalized shame and victim-blaming that impede healing. We can all work together to reduce rape culture and victim-blaming, and improve resources for survivors. Survivors can share hopeful narratives of bearing witness to our truth.

"My body knows what to do." During a rape or other assault, it is common for the body to freeze until the assault is over. This is a source of shame-filled narratives like, "My body betrayed me. I didn't fight hard enough." Similarly, it is common for trans people to stay silently closeted until there is enough safety (or desperation) to come out.

Try a new narrative: "I survived. My body knew what to do. Freezing is a completely normal response to danger."

In an emergency, the body has powerful impulses to *do something*. We go into freeze as a last-ditch attempt to survive when the danger is too big and overwhelming, or our possible actions conflict with each other, or we have the habit of freezing from earlier emergencies. That powerful energy arises during the thawing and healing process, leading to the narrative, "I'm frozen. I have to do something!"

Try a new narrative: "Freeze is self-limiting. In a safe environment, all I have to do is let the freeze be there, and my body will come out of it in time." It is normal to come out of freeze the way we went in, terrified or furious or desperate for help. With kind attention, the feelings will resolve.

Reach for hope. Whenever you find yourself thinking that you are crazy and wrong and bad, try a new narrative: "My perceptions and responses make sense. I am intrinsically good. I am doing my best with the resources and knowledge I have."

Whenever you find yourself thinking that nothing will ever change, remember that "never" and "forever" are flashback markers. Flashbacks are memories that are frozen in time. Try a new narrative: "Change is possible." The present might already be moving toward the change you seek. You might make a new friend, read a new book or blog post, or find some other source of new ideas. A bigger shift might change everything. Allow yourself to reach for hope.

Naomi's update. In 2020, Naomi Ceder reports that she recently completed three years as the chair of the Python Software Foundation. "That was a narrative option I didn't have four years ago, being a trans woman leading the organization that manages the community of one of the top three programming languages on earth. I still find that somewhat incredible, but every few months I do hear from trans people (women and men) who tell me that my example has given them a narrative that they didn't have before, and that it has helped them. And that makes me happy indeed."

She notes that her story also resonates with cisgender women, perhaps as encouragement to find an alternative to society's confining expectations. She continues, "It may also be that in a way my story affirms the value of being a woman – I would certainly like to think it does, and heaven knows I struggled enough to get there. It's only implicit in that talk, but the other negative narrative I had to change to move forward was the misogynistic one I learned from society (my mother in particular, ironically). Reading and embracing feminism was a key component in my finding that narrative."*

---

* Private communication, November 8, 2020, quoted with permission.

Consider Additional Truths

Ideally, as we grow up we learn to balance consideration for others with consideration for ourselves, regardless of gender roles. We see the adults around us treating others and themselves with care. We experience being treated with care. We are directly taught to lift our attention from our immediate concerns to include the concerns and narratives of the people around us.

Unbalanced priorities. Some kids (more likely for those raised as girls) are taught to be considerate of others to the exclusion of their own well-being. They are told their value comes from making others comfortable. They learn the emotional labor skills of paying attention to subtle signals and imagining how others might feel. Making themselves a priority in any way is called "selfish" and "bad."

Some kids (more likely for those raised as boys) are taught that prioritizing themselves is the way to win. They are told their value comes from getting ahead and getting what they want. They can succeed despite or perhaps because of their obliviousness. They take consideration from others for granted.

In abusive households, kids learn a terrified attentiveness to the abuser's moods and movements. They strain to sense any information that might help them stay unnoticed and unhurt. They learn to placate others and conceal their needs. Abuse itself is a profound lack of consideration for the victim's well-being.

Equality and respect. As adults, we might find ourselves in any or all of those roles at different times: erasing ourselves, erasing others, placating someone with more power, or hurting someone with less power. In contrast, consideration comes from a place of equality and respect. We are all humans together and we can make each other's lives a little easier by being mindful of more than our own priorities. When we have more power and privilege, it is our job to be more considerate of those who have less.

Consideration starts with compassion for ourselves. If we are contemptuous toward our weaknesses and needs, we are likely to bring the same attitude toward others. When we help someone while looking down on them, the recipient is likely to feel uncomfortable even if they are not sure why.

Anchored in our story. To be considerate of ourselves, we anchor ourselves in our story. We believe our present experience, including when we feel confusion and doubt. We believe our memories, allowing them to be solid or hazy, coherent or fragmentary. We believe our sensitivities and take action to meet our physical needs. We bring patience and understanding to our imperfections and mistakes and after-effects of trauma. We care for ourselves as best we can with the knowledge and resources we have.

We turn toward ourselves with kindness, including all our conflicting opinions and impulses and wants. We hear the overall truth of our experience, and allow additional truths to emerge. Perhaps we have always hated exercise and movement, and at the same time we sense curiosity about aqua aerobics. Perhaps we have always yielded our time to care for others, and now we are determined to take that art class. Perhaps we have always moved forward into each challenge, and something inside longs to pause, retreat, and rest.

Stay curious. To be considerate of other people, we remember that they are just that: separate people, each with their story and perspective. They are not backdrops or props for our unfolding story. We turn toward them with the same respect we bring toward ourselves.

What we know and what others know only partly overlaps. No matter how well-informed we are, there are whole areas of knowledge and experience that we have never imagined. We stay curious about the truth of other people's experiences, and listen with care. We hold the knowledge that they are human just as we are, and at the same time, we do not know their internal truths unless they tell us.

Share our truths. Sometimes we can ease the way for others by sharing our truths. So much is uncertain and stressful in everyone's lives. We can bridge the gaps of not-knowing and alleviate uncertainty in small practical ways by texting when we are running late, or by offering a timely response when someone has shared a vulnerable truth, or by sharing our vulnerable truths or expertise.

At the same time, we stay aware of whether our sharing is wanted. One of the most considerate things we can do is assume that these independent beings around us can competently manage their lives as they see fit. People do not need or want unsolicited advice or assistance.

Ask. In particular, people with disabilities and chronic illnesses have skillfully adapted to their circumstances. Ask before "helping," and listen to the response. For example, people using wheelchairs definitely do not want a surprise push, and might not want a door held either. Consideration can be about stepping back rather than fulfilling our need to feel useful.

In general, we can be more considerate by keeping our

minds and our senses open to input. The more we sense into our present environment and the people around us with caring, the less we impose our world view on others. We can directly ask what others need when the signals are not clear, and believe what they tell us.

Affirming antidote. It is draining to move through the world in a considerate way without receiving consideration in return. It takes energy to decide when and how to speak up after being erased, and it is demoralizing to have to remind people, "Hey, I'm a person!" It is even worse when others respond angrily to being reminded.

It can be a form of gaslighting to have our point of view so thoroughly ignored that we wonder if it exists at all. The antidote is hearing affirmation. "I see you. That makes sense. Of course you feel that way!" Children build up the skill of self-affirmation by receiving abundant affirmation from the adults around them. People who missed out on that will be more strongly affected by having their point of view erased in the present.

Return to consideration. We can all be oblivious at times, caught up in our story and not realizing how we affect others. When we remember to bring more consideration to our truths and those of the people around us, we bring more ease and healing to the world.

Offer a Collaborative Story

Jacinta realized she was angry because her point of view had been erased. She said to her friend Reya, "I'm mad about our translation project. I still think this idiom isn't quite right."

Reya said flatly, "I disagree."

Jacinta took a deep breath and tried again. "I really appreciate that you did this translation. Your technical Spanish is much better than mine, and I'm grateful for your work. I thought we were collaborating. What I can contribute is fixing this one sentence that sounds jarring to my ear. You're throwing away my contribution."

Reya softened. "Oh. That's a much better story than mine. I thought you were saying I was wrong." Together they fixed the translation.

Facing a wall. It can be puzzling and infuriating when someone repeatedly does not consider our point of view. "You're not listening!" rarely goes over well, but it is hard to know what else to say when we face a blank wall.

Reya was caught up in an old story that did not have room for Jacinta's contribution. Sometimes our shame or fear is too loud to let us hear someone else's message. Jacinta took a step back and named her experience without blaming or ascribing negative motives. Her underlying message was, "I want us to be on the same side." Fortunately, Reya could hear and accept her invitation.

Your perspective. When you find yourself facing a blank wall, take some time away from the conversation to find a collaborative story.

First, stand firmly in your story. Make room for your emotions and perspective. It makes sense to be angry, confused, or upset when you are not heard. Acknowledge any shame or fear that comes up. Affirm that you get to have a point of view, separately from being judged right or wrong.

Best outcome. What is the best outcome you would like to see? Jacinta wanted to address a specific task and generally repair their friendship. Desired outcomes might also include peaceful coexistence, acknowledgement, validation, clarifying boundaries, and communicating feedback.

Patterns. If the situation reminds you of past experiences, look at both similarities and differences in yourself and in the situation. Your collaborative story can acknowledge the similarities to the past, and the new outcome you would like to see.

If you find yourself behaving in ways that are not usual for you, acknowledge that too. Sometimes we get pulled into a role in someone else's story. We all tend to project our pasts and expectations on present events.

Their perspective. Now turn your attention to the other person's story. Imagine how the situation looks from their point of view. Even though we tend to assume people are judging us, it might not be about you at all. Are there times that you have acted the way they are acting? See them with compassion as a vulnerable human trying to meet needs and avoid pain. What do you genuinely appreciate about them?

Return to your story and point of view. Has it changed after visiting the other person's perspective? Can you imagine a perspective that puts you both on the same side? While you see them as an enemy, you will not be able to offer a collaborative story.

Offer your story. Note that a collaborative story includes everyone's full emotions, perspectives, and boundaries. You do not have to erase parts of yourself to collaborate. Put together a brief story that conveys, "I see and respect you as a fellow struggling human. This is what is happening for me. Here is the collaborative outcome I want. Can we address this together?" In an ongoing conflict, it might help to explicitly explore everyone's underlying stories.

Find a time to offer your collaborative story and then listen for their response and their story. You may feel the relief and softening of being heard, or you may continue to feel the frustration of being blocked out. Sometimes people remain committed to their competitive or combative story despite your offer of collaboration. Listening for their story might give them an opportunity to disengage from defensiveness.

Center marginalized viewpoints. People who are immersed in their point of view might only need a gentle reminder to consider yours as well. Unfortunately, sometimes people remain persistently oblivious to others' points of view.

When someone resembles their society's "default human" (able-bodied, cis, straight, white, male, Christian, etc.), they are surrounded by narratives reinforcing their point of view. By contrast, someone with a more marginalized identity constantly practices understanding both the mainstream point of view and their own. We can all benefit from decentering mainstream stories and listening to more marginalized viewpoints.

Trauma effects can also play a role. Dissociation leads people to shut down awareness of the outside world. Hypervigilance leads people to attend to every nuance of the people around them. People who have been subject to emotional abuse tend to reflexively question their point of view even when no one else is currently invalidating it.

Monitor emotional labor. It takes emotional labor to find and offer collaborative stories in the face of ongoing blank walls. When someone repeatedly shuts out your point of view, you can monitor whether the relationship is sustainable for you.

Inner voices. Collaborative stories can help ease conflicts with inner parts as well. Even the most negative internal parts are fundamentally trying to help us survive, possibly with outdated information and tools. Over time, we learn to listen for their stories with compassion, enabling inner voices to work together to survive and thrive in the present.

Invite connection. Loneliness and depression are endemic. When we invite people to be on the same side with collaborative stories, we open the door to more connection in our lives.

Practice Kind Language

Content Note: Ableist language used as negative examples.

As we walked along, my friend tripped over a raised bit of sidewalk. "Pick up your feet!" she scolded herself. I could imagine her four-year-old self being dragged by the hand as her mother scolded her in exactly those words a half-century earlier.

Oppression by default. We absorb the language that we hear around us. Until we consciously and considerately choose new patterns, we spit out the same language, unchanged. Without thinking about the implications, we use phrases that support and perpetuate oppressive narratives. "It took balls to say that," associates courage with cis men. "That's so gay!" said with disdain, reinforces rigid gender roles and encourages anti-gay bullying.

Kind language gives us building blocks for kinder narratives for ourselves and others.

Ableist language. We absorb a lot of ableist language, which associates negative traits with disabilities. Having a disability is not inherently negative, despite the obstacles society places in a disabled person's way. People with disabilities have the full gamut of positive, neutral, and negative human qualities. Any of us could become (more) disabled at any time through injury, illness, or aging.

"She was blind to the consequences," implies that blind people do not pay attention. In truth, people with visual impairments have to pay more careful attention than most to navigate the world. We can say, "She ignored the consequences," or "She did not consider the consequences."

"That's lame," to express "uncool" or "a poor effort" wrongly associates those qualities with people who limp or have other mobility impairments. We can find a way to criticize someone's effort with more precision, if we need to be critical at all.

Respect intellectual disabilities. People with intellectual disabilities are a common target. Mistakes and questions are not "stupid," although they might be thoughtless or unwise. Rather than equating more intellectual capacity with more value, we can give people with intellectual disabilities our full respect and stop insulting people by calling them "moron," "idiot," and so on. "Dumb" means unable to speak and is also ableist when used as an insult.

Crazy does not mean bad. Another common ableist word is "crazy," along with its many synonyms like "insane" and "nuts." We sprinkle them liberally into our conversation to mean unreliable, excessive, chaotic, socially unacceptable, or violent, which directly associates mental illness with those qualities.

Mental illness does not make it more likely that someone will commit violence.* In fact, people living with mental illness are more likely than others to be victims of violence. Shooting up a school or concert hall with an assault rifle is wrong, destructive, and evil. It is not "crazy." Abusers are abusive, cruel, unethical, mean, manipulative—not "crazy."

We use "crazy" as a slur to discredit and devalue people

---

* "Fact vs. myth: mental health issues & violence."
https://sane.org/information-stories/facts-and-guides/fvm-mental-illness-and-violence

who are mentally ill, as well as people whose behavior we disapprove of, such as assertive, independent women. We criticize ideas that are new to us by calling them "crazy," rather than calling them "puzzling," "unusual," "startling," or "contrary to facts as we know them."

Positive uses of crazy. "Crazed" originally meant "filled with random cracks," like some glazes on ceramic pieces. We can continue to use it in that sense.

People with PTSD, anxiety, depression, or other mental illnesses can choose to reclaim the word to refer to themselves.

Too little and too much. Avoiding ableist language might seem like a trivial action that barely moves the needle. At the same time, it is a concrete step we can take to make a difference in both ourselves and our culture. If everyone made a commitment to use kind, non-oppressive language, we would give welcome breathing space to marginalized groups and interrupt subconscious reinforcement of oppression.

Avoiding ableist language might also seem overwhelming, choking off spontaneity and adding yet another reason for shame and self-criticism.

Work in progress. When we frame our language changes as a practice, we acknowledge up front that we are imperfect works in progress. We can approach the effort to change our language with kindness, one word at a time.

The first step is observation and awareness. We simply notice how we and the people around us use the word we selected. We might be surprised by the frequency and taken aback by the hidden judgments that surface.

When we are ready to take action, we can think of specific alternatives in advance. When the unwanted word pops out of our mouth, we can correct ourselves out loud and move on. "Blind … I mean oblivious." We can also pause in conversation while we search for a non-ableist word to express our thoughts. When we visibly pause and correct ourselves, we provide others with a positive role model.

In time, the corrections will happen smoothly before we speak, and we can choose a new word to practice with.

Interventions. When someone else uses ableist language, we can quietly offer an alternative. "The store was crazy today!" "It was busy?"

When we are in charge of a space and someone uses offensive words, we can say, "We don't do that here."*

When we practice kind language externally, we also practice to be kinder to ourselves internally. We can use the same gentle retraining with our Inner Critic. "That was a crazy thing to say!" "Maybe it didn't make sense…" "You idiot!" "We don't do that here." We all need room to be imperfect humans, internally and externally.

Suspend judgment. A lot of our ableist language not only mistakenly assumes that people with disabilities are generally damaged or broken, it also leaps to conclusions about the specific person in front of us. Behavior that looks "crazy" (nonsensical) or "stupid" (thoughtless) from the outside might make perfect sense with more information. Even when behavior may be caused by mental illness or intellectual disability, none of us are licensed to diagnose people outside a clinical setting.

We can suspend judgment and assume that people are managing their lives in a way that works for them. When we change our language, it supports more positive narratives about the people around us.

---

* "We Don't Do That Here" by Aja Hammerly, September 29, 2017. https://thagomizer.com/blog/2017/09/29/we-don-t-do-that-here.html

Relieve Pressure: Replace Should With Could

When we simultaneously feel that we "should" get a lot of paying work done and "should" do self-care and "should" maintain a clean home and "should" make the world a better place, we feel shame about failing in so many ways. Create kinder narratives by replacing "should" with "could." "Should" makes us look over our shoulder to see if we are good enough yet. "Could" invites us to look inside instead.

We can only do one thing at a time. When we choose what to do next, we could do paying work or self-care or home maintenance or activism. Perhaps we do want to make progress on a project or do the dishes to fulfill commitments made by our past self, or as a gift to our future self.

More possibilities. Where "should" narrows the field and already knows the right answer, "could" adds possibilities and questions. Is it true that we could do that? We all have limits, both internally and externally. Perhaps washing dishes would trigger back pain. Perhaps paying work is much harder to find as a Black woman. Do we want to do that? Perhaps our intuition senses that an opportunity we "should" take would not be good for us.

We might want to do something that is not included in that list of "shoulds." We could do something fun, or sit down and rest. Perhaps we have emotions that need our kind attention before we can take action.

We might feel overwhelmed by a task we want to get done.

We could ask for help. We could take a tiny step that seems too small to count, like washing a single dish, or looking up a phone number, or opening a document. Tiny steps still move forward, and might be the only way to make progress on an intimidating task.

Internalized voices. In an effort to be a good person and to win others' approval, we tell ourselves what we "should" be doing, the experiences we "should" be having, and the trajectories our lives "should" be taking.

As children, we internalize adults' voices and absorb what we "should" do and how we "should" be from media and advertisements. That mainstream narrative might not apply. We could consciously change the internal committee that tells us what is right and wrong. We could affirm to ourselves that we are already enough, just as we are right now.

External "shoulds." In the present, when someone says, "You should…" we can hear it as, "You could…" or "I want you to…". When people give us advice, they are talking about their own life and experience. We can nod politely and consider whether it applies to us.

When a friend says, "You should watch this movie with me," they might mean, "It's a great movie and I think you would enjoy it." When you pause to consider whether you want to join them, they easily accept your answer.

On the other hand, they might mean, "I don't want to watch it alone, so I'm going to push you to join me." In that case, they might use increasing fear, obligation, and guilt to pressure you into accompanying them.

Sticking to "could" helps you take a step back from their pressure. You can pause to evaluate how their agenda affects you, and whether you want to go along with part or all of it. Maybe you do want to keep them company even though you had other plans. Maybe you want to offer an alternative activity for the evening. Maybe you want to give a firm, clear, "No," despite feeling guilty.

Resolving guilt. We reflexively avoid the pain of feeling guilty. We can inquire inside whether we feel appropriate guilt because our behavior did not meet our own standards. If so, we can resolve it by looking at how to do better next time, apologizing, and making amends as best we can. When the friend says, "You promised you would watch with me!" you could respond, "I'm sorry. I messed up. I'll be more careful with what I promise in the future."

We can decline to feel or engage with guilt if we were doing our best, or we are taking on too much responsibility that is not ours, or we already tried to make amends. We can think the magic words, "Not my problem." The Polish version is, "Not my circus, not my monkeys." Nie mój cyrk, nie moje małpy.

If you had made it clear that you probably would not watch the movie, you might say to the friend, "I hear that you are disappointed. I hope you find someone to watch with you or have a good time on your own," and kindly end the conversation.

Values and ethics. Sometimes we use "should" to mean, "The world should work this way according to my values and ethics." For example, when we see someone harassing a woman who is wearing hijab, we think, "Someone should do something. That shouldn't be happening." We make a personal choice between "Not my problem," or "Too dangerous to intervene," or "I am someone. I will do something."

We could say out loud, "That's not okay," or provide quiet support by sitting down next to her and striking up a conversation about the weather. When one person takes a small action, other observers are more likely to take action as well.

While we absorb values and ethics from the people and culture around us, we also have a responsibility to evaluate how we want to behave, and what world we want to help create.

Choices and boundaries. Each day, we work toward living in agreement with our chosen values and ethics. While our Inner Critic and people around us will continue to pile on the "shoulds," we can respond with self-compassion and self-forgiveness when our daily efforts fall short of our aspirations. Replacing "should" with "could" relieves painful pressure and gives us more room to make clear choices.

Good Enough for Mistakes

How do you respond when you make a mistake? Do you take it in stride? Crumple in shame? Panic? Do you tell yourself you "should" have done better? What we count as a mistake and how we respond depends on our current resources and the narratives around mistakes as we grew up.

Inexperience. Children naturally make a lot of mistakes. As we grow, our main task is to acquire experience about the world, and experience comes from trying things that we have not completely figured out. Adults who are learning and growing make mistakes too.

Inattentiveness. Mistakes can also come from inattentiveness. There is a relaxed middle ground between hypervigilance to make sure everything is done perfectly on one end, and habitually expecting others to bear the brunt of our lack of care at the other end. Inattentiveness could be caused by tiredness, dissociation, brain fog from sensitivities or illness, and/or substance use.

Risks. We often call it a mistake if a risk does not work out the way we wanted, or if we fail to predict unexpected consequences of an action. Taking risks is part of living, whether we tend to take smaller risks or larger ones. We can let ourselves off the hook for not being able to predict or control the future. Risks can lead to unexpectedly good outcomes as well as unexpectedly bad ones.

In environments where small mistakes can have dangerous consequences such as winter camping or using power tools, we stay aware of our actions, double-check everything, and prepare as best we can for unexpected events.

Resources. A small mistake for one person might be a huge mistake for someone else, depending on their available resources. One person might get a parking ticket, shrug, and pay it. Another person might pay it and then yell at themselves for days about not seeing the No Parking sign. Another person might not have the funds to pay and start a downward spiral of escalating fees, vehicle impoundment, losing their job, and losing their housing. We all deserve a safety net to help us recover from mistakes.

People with more privilege tend to be seen as more capable by default. They are given more leeway for mistakes and more help in recovering from them. People with privilege often do not realize what is behind their "good luck."

Repair. In a safe environment, small mistakes are mostly allowed to go by, and big mistakes are discussed with a focus on the behavior rather than the person. There might be teaching about better ways to handle similar situations in the future. There might be communication about the consequences of the mistake, including anger or grief.

When we make a mistake, we can repair it by listening, apologizing, and making amends where possible. We can think about why the mistake occurred, perhaps asking several layers of "why?" to discover underlying causes, and put effort into avoiding that mistake in the future. We can forgive ourselves for being human and making mistakes.

Abusive responses. In an abusive environment, any misstep can be seized as an excuse for verbal abuse or violence. Even though responsibility for abuse lies with the abuser, we walk on eggshells and try to "do it right" to keep the abuser calm. Mistakes might be brought up accusingly for years rather than being repaired and laid to rest.

Another abusive pattern is "mistakes" that are ongoing boundary violations. While we all make mistakes, it is an act of aggression to keep making the same mistakes without immediate efforts to correct or compensate for the problem. We can make room for genuine mistakes, and continue to expect respectful treatment.

If we have lived in safe environments, we internalize a warm, forgiving response to our mistakes. In abusive environments, we internalize accusatory responses instead. Our Inner Critic might vividly replay old mistakes, bringing a flood of shame.

Worried critical voice. As part of Inner Relationship Focusing, Ann Weiser Cornell and Barbara McGavin frame internal criticism as two voices plus a larger self: a part that is criticizing, a part that is receiving the criticism, and the larger witness self that accompanies and includes them both.*

They suggest that the critical inner voice might be worried or concerned about something, and that it is often trying to protect us, even if the tactics are unpleasant. For example, a parent who yells, "You'll get run over!" wants their child to cross the street carefully and safely. We can kindly ask inside whether the critical voice is worried, and what it is trying to prevent.

When a critical inner voice brings up an embarrassing memory, this framing gives us breathing room to be curious and compassionate, rather than overwhelmed with shame. While it might seem random or spontaneous, there was a reason that particular memory came up. We can look back to

---

* "Radical Gentleness: The Transformation of the Inner Critic" by Ann Weiser Cornell. https://focusingresources.com/radical-gentleness-the-transformation-of-the-inner-critic/

see if there was a cascade of thoughts or a bodily sensation or a recent event that brought it to mind.

Every time we turn toward an inner emotion, memory, or experience with kindness and compassion, we are strengthening that larger witness self. Our inner parts can relax into that encompassing companionship, rather than struggling with overwhelming events while feeling small and alone.

Confident recovery. When we live in fear and lack resources, we tighten up against mistakes. When we emerge from the urgency and panic of trauma responses to feel flexible, playful, courageous, and confident, we can use our skills and resources to recover from mistakes and integrate them into the flow of life.

We can say, "I'm sorry. Let me repair this," rather than shutting down or fleeing. While we might try to be good enough by never making mistakes, knowing we are already good enough is a foundation that supports mistakes and recovery.

1: Wider Narratives

Loosen Inner Deadlock

As we navigate life's choices, we usually reach a decision by a combination of checking inside ourselves, researching options, asking others for advice, and flipping a coin. Sometimes none of that works and we find ourselves deadlocked, unable to settle on a resolution, fearful of making a mistake.

An inner deadlock can manifest as an intense battle with constant internal arguments, or instead as numbness and shutting down, when we want to do something but it is simply not happening. In that case, some part is silently resisting rather than arguing. We can find a way forward with a wider narrative that includes all our partial perspectives.

Our Inner Critic is often a big player in deadlocks, telling us we "should" be decisive and clear, and at the same time telling us our reasons are not good enough when we reach a tentative conclusion. When our trust in our internal perceptions and assessments has been undermined, we lose our foundation for making decisions that work well for us.

Mali's deadlock. For example, Mali (who uses they/them pronouns) is trying to decide whether to take an evening class they have been eyeing for a long time. They feel pushed to take the class now, and overwhelmed by the extra time and work involved. They keep thinking about it and talking it over with friends, and neither answer feels right.

Add time and space. When you notice an internal deadlock, it helps to decrease the urgency and intensity of the conflict by adding more time and space. If there is imminent danger, then take emergency action. Otherwise, take some time to notice your current environment and current safety. Invite your body to breathe and settle. You will find a way through, one way or another.

Is there a way to make the looming decision smaller in scope, or reduce time pressure? Most opportunities will come around again, and might be a better fit in the future. Perhaps you can try out a decision for a limited time to gather more information about what does and does not work for you. Check for exits and off ramps, ways to change your mind if needed.

Separate parts. You can create a Decision-Free Zone to listen to all of yourself with a clear boundary that action is off the table. As you learn more, you might discover that there are more than two conflicting parts involved, or that two conflicting parts have the same agenda or concern underneath.

If parts are too busy contradicting each other to explore why they feel the way they do, try separating them. Assign each part a separate place in the room, still included, but at a small distance. You get space in the center to sense how you feel when you get a break from conflict.

Mali puts the pressure to take the class on one side, and the feeling of being overwhelmed on the other. They pause to enjoy relief from the constant internal struggle. When they turn toward the feeling of overwhelm, they remember that they have been fighting off a cold for a couple of weeks and feel tired all the time. No wonder taking a class sounds like too much work. They also touch into a deeper need for rest and open time.

When Mali turns toward the sense of pressure, they realize they are still hearing their mother's voice saying, "You do nothing but sit at home. You have to get out and do things and meet people!" Mali has always needed more quiet alone time than their extroverted mother, and their mother does not acknowledge the difference in their needs.

While it can be helpful to consider a variety of opinions, other people do not necessarily know what is right for us. It can ease a deadlock to separate your own voice from other people's present and past opinions.

Allow imperfection. If you feel required to find a perfect answer that pleases everyone, spend some time with the part that feels that way. Listen for what that part is worried will happen if your choice is not exactly right. Let the part know you hear it, and let it rest into your support and warmth. If parts come up that want to argue, correct, or reassure another part, let them know you hear them, too.

As you try to predict what will work for you in the future, remind yourself that risks and mistakes are part of learning and growing. You can also check whether something inside is worried about limited resources.

Limits and needs. Healing from trauma can increase our resilience, giving us a wider range of tools and skills and experiences. Trauma also erodes our inner resources, narrowing our window of tolerance for stress and mistakes. An irritated nervous system needs protection and care. Like other injuries, illnesses, and disabilities, PTSD imposes limits that can be frustrating. We might strongly want to move forward, and also strongly need to rest.

Questioning the validity of each internal opinion and need intensifies a deadlock. Deeply listening to each voice loosens the knots rather than tightening them. Instead of investigating whether a response comes out of the past or the present, fully acknowledge that you hear it. Give yourself room to be affected by the past.

Calm company. If you hear from a terrified inner child, give them company for their terror, with the calm adult presence they have been waiting for. If a part wants to shame or scold the child, ask that part to talk to your adult self instead. Look for experiences of calm accompaniment in your past and your present to support you.

Give yourself as much compassion as you can for your experience of deadlock. You are not alone in your struggles. We all experience powerful needs, stubborn resistance, and inner deadlocks.

Bring some curiosity to the deadlock itself. Perhaps it is part of a recurring pattern. It is hard to decide what to do when every option is part of the pattern. As you learn about all the different parts that contribute to the pattern, you can gradually find a wider perspective that leads to both/and solutions rather than either/or choices.

As Mali sits with their parts, they find more compassion for their need for rest and quiet. They also notice an underlying goal to connect more positively with their mother. Rather than taking the class, Mali tentatively reaches out. If their mother pushes them to do more, they lightly push back, change the subject, or leave the conversation. Fortunately, their mother gets the point quickly, and their relationship improves.

Inclusive solutions. The surface issue of a deadlock might seem easy to resolve by "just" deciding one way or the other. As we explore more deeply, we see the full complexity of parts and tensions between them. We can loosen those tensions by giving each part room to express its needs and fears, creating a wider narrative. Inclusive solutions gradually emerge as we gain understanding of the whole situation.

Resources

An ultimately hopeful animated 9 min. video. "A Message From the Future II: The Years of Repair," art by Molly Crabapple, political storytelling by Naomi Klein, Avi Lewis, and Opal Tometi. https://youtu.be/2m8YACFJlMg

Active Hope, New World Library, 2012, by Joanna Macy and Chris Johnstone gives practical steps for living the story of the Great Turning toward sustainable lives.

Hope in the Dark, Haymarket Books, 2016, by Rebecca Solnit describes how change happens at the margins, slowly, then all at once. We quickly forget the long battles that have already been won, especially environmental battles where victory leaves a region unchanged.

The Newcomers: Finding Refuge, Friendship, and Hope in an American Classroom, Simon and Schuster Trade, 2018, by Helen Thorpe is the true story of a class of teen refugee English Language Learners in Denver, Colorado, told with clarity and compassion.

Embodying Hope

2: Difficult Times

How can we find hope in difficult times without resorting to denial or pretense? To start, we can honor all our responses, whether from the past or the present. We can name what is the same and what is different between traumatic back then and challenging right now.

We struggle with not being able to control distressing events, and at the same time we are not helpless and alone the way we may have been during past trauma. We can connect with others to talk about our experiences and create a way forward together. Our current difficulties may be new to us, but many people have found their way through similar difficulties in the past.

We can recognize our agency to choose our responses and give ourselves time to adapt to abrupt changes and ongoing crises such as the Covid-19 pandemic.

As trauma survivors, we lacked protection in the past, and

we often have challenges around belonging in the present. We can be with those longings, and find belonging in our choices to act for the greater good.

White supremacy and systemic racism have been inflicting difficult times and trauma on BIPOC (Black, Indigenous, and People of Color) for centuries. White people are also harmed. We can all work toward a better world by seeing racism and talking about it.

We can make choices about the information and stories we take in and make sure we are hearing good news in addition to the latest disasters. Even in difficult times, people are taking positive action, and we can join them. Amid the clamor of urgency and panic, we can each find sustainable avenues of resistance.

We embody hope by continuing to live and care for one another, one moment at a time.

Withstand Ongoing Trauma

After trauma is over, "It ended!" is a powerful healing tool to convince your body that the emergency is over. What happens when the trauma, or similar threats, are ongoing?

The ongoing threat might be fearing a boss or leader who resembles the unpredictable, vindictive, bullying, sexually abusive head of household from childhood. Grieving the latest person pulled over and murdered for Driving While Black. Flinching at another text from a stalking ex-spouse. Gasping at a letter saying already minimal disability benefits will be cut further. Feeling personally targeted for being a woman, or queer, or trans, or Muslim, or Jewish. Watching the death count rise from an uncontrolled pandemic.

Validation. Amid news reports and conversations that make light of bizarre events or frankly contradict them, it helps to talk with people who simply acknowledge reality. Yes, this is happening. No, this is not normal.

Your reactions are valid. All of them. You get to feel aching grief, like being kicked in the chest. You get to feel liquid rage. You get to feel terrified by historical parallels and growing present-time threats. You get to be numb, frozen. You get to throw yourself into action and activism. You get to alternate among many reactions.

Separate past from present. You get to be triggered by current events, responding with the terror and helplessness of a child. It helps when you can kindly recognize that you are triggered, finding your inner witness who says, "I feel terrible. I wonder which parts of this are old." Let your child self know that you are listening, and that you feel the terror and helplessness.

As terrifying as the present may be, it is not a replay of childhood abuse. To find your larger witness self, remind yourself of today's date and your current age. Push long with your feet and wide with your elbows to feel your full adult size and strength. Name aloud resources you have now that you did not have as a child, for example a bank account, driver's license, more years of experience, and more connections with other people. Look around at your current environment, and name what is different from the past.

Connection and touch. Amid violent, dehumanizing rhetoric and actions, it helps to be in conversation with someone who responds to you as the living breathing valuable being you are. Positive connection is a balm in hard times. You can connect with other people, with pets, with Nature, and even with yourself. Look yourself in the eye in the mirror and say, "You matter."

Remember that the people around you are going through their own reactions and may not be available for connection when you ask. Keep reaching out.

Safe touch can directly calm the nervous system. I worked on a lot of clients' feet after the shocking US election result in 2016, soothing muscle and contacting bone. It helps to remember that your body is still there, and feel its edges.*

Familiar routine. As much as you can, continue with your daily routine, especially self-care like meals and sleep. As you navigate change, your body appreciates familiar patterns.

---

* See "The Push/Pull of Touch" on page 140 for gentle non-sexual self-touch suggestions.

You may feel like cocooning alone, or you may want people around you all the time. Consider attending your regular group activities even if it takes extra energy. Even if it has to be online during a pandemic. Participate in something that takes your whole attention and distracts you for a while.

Stillness and motion. Give yourself a few minutes to sit still, perhaps in meditation or over a cup of tea. Allow yourself to connect with what is happening inside you. It might be uncomfortable or unexpected, and at the same time, the distress and other reactions inside like to be heard and acknowledged.

Give yourself time to walk or bike outside. Notice the details of the weather and the changing season today. How does the air feel? Balmy, chilly, sharp? How does it smell? The world is still turning. Plants are growing, or lying dormant for the winter. Small creatures rustle through leaves, gather seeds, rest and play.

Thinnest slice of now. When events are huge and overwhelming, give yourself a break by focusing just on what is happening now, rather than including everything that is coming in the future. Right now, you are breathing in and out. In this moment, you are safe from harassment.

Robyn Posin names this "focusing on the thinnest slice of now,"* and reminds us that even though we feel overwhelmed, our future self may well have more resources to handle future events. At least, our future self will have had more time to adapt to sudden changes and disasters.

Best case, worst case. While it helps to focus on the present, we do want to put some time and energy into planning for the future. When we look at both best and worst cases, it

---

* "Change Moving Quickly" by Robyn Posin.
http://forthelittleonesinside.com/4change-moving-quickly

reminds us that we do not yet know what will happen, and allows us to make more flexible plans.

Take some time to acknowledge your fears of the worst case. What are you afraid of losing? What are you afraid of experiencing? Acknowledge your fears and give them some space. If you think of concrete steps you could take to protect yourself from bad outcomes, just note them for now.

Also spend some time with best outcomes. Find outcomes that bring relief. Maybe an ally steps in. Maybe new facts come to light that change the whole situation. Breathe in the relief. In times of not-knowing, allow yourself some time with relief. Do any concrete steps come to mind to make a good outcome more likely?

Choose action. From your contemplation of best and worst cases, from talking with others, from listening to your body, from any other ideas that float up, choose at least one action.

Waiting is also a valid choice. Allow yourself time to be with shock and confusion, which are reasonable responses to shocking and confusing events. Allow yourself time to observe and learn, and move into action when you see an opportunity that is a good fit for you.

Remember resilience. What resilient strategies have you inherited? What strategies have you developed for yourself? What has helped you survive this long? As you move through difficult, triggering events in the present, bring along all the healing tools you have already collected.

Agency in a Time of Pandemic

In difficult times, our resilience is supported by perceiving our agency: the capacity to take action.

We are individually and collectively learning how to live in a worldwide pandemic. We are adapting to disorienting change at the same time as managing our emotional responses to this crisis. As pandemic waves move toward us disarmingly slowly and then shockingly fast in their exponential growth pattern*, we each move from initial denial and resistance through uncertainty and confusion to reluctant acceptance and protective action.

Ability to act. We support our agency when we own our skills and knowledge. A sense of agency says, "I may not know what to do yet, but I will figure it out." Agency includes small stubborn steps, not just flashy victories. When we discern what we can and cannot change in the moment, we can make powerful choices within ourselves to wait or remain silent or endure discomfort when in other circumstances we would leave or speak out or fight back. Agency includes patiently planning and working toward a future when we can actively move forward.

This pandemic is not something we can fix or control. We can strive to do everything right, and we might still get sick. People we love might get sick. Illness is not a punishment. We are each making decisions about risks and trade-offs as

---

* "Exponential Growth and Epidemics" by Grant Sanderson, 9 minute explanatory video. https://youtu.be/Kas0tIxDvrg

best we can. When we feel stuck, we can listen to all sides of an inner deadlock about what to do. We can acknowledge places where our choices are externally limited, for example people who work in essential jobs with insufficient protection and pay because they need to make rent.

Staying home is heroic. If you are out providing essential services, it is easier to see your agency and heroic contributions. For many people, agency in this pandemic is quieter. Washing hands. Staying home. Learning how to teach and study and work online. Remember that those quiet actions are equally heroic. Your choices are directly saving lives.

Staying home has its challenges. It can trigger memories of past times at home, including being trapped with an abusive parent or partner. You can practice noticing same and different to help distinguish the past from the present. Name a couple of things that are the same, and a couple of things that are different. Take note of your current strengths and capacities and choices.

If you are staying home or working in a job with someone who is behaving abusively in the present, reach out for support to make a safety plan.*

New routines. Sudden change has its challenges. It takes more energy to do things in new ways. Keep as many of your routines as you can, and give yourself time to build new ones. Be kind to yourself around food and eating, especially if you are used to eating out or shopping often.

If you find yourself with unexpected free time while sheltering in place, ask yourself what you enjoy. Make a list of

---

* A safety plan is a personalized, practical plan to improve your safety while experiencing abuse, preparing to leave an abusive situation, or after you leave. Checklists and resources: https://calltosafety.org/services/safety-planning/

creative and repair projects you might want to tackle and skills you want to learn. Is there a musical instrument in your closet or a language you want to work on?

Have compassion for your body and nervous system that are busy creating new routines and processing anxiety, fear, and grief. You may be less focused, less efficient, more forgetful, or more clumsy than usual. Your first need might be for rest, a need that is often unmet in a fast-paced life.

Have compassion for the people around you who are going through similar processes in their own way. As much as you can, offer understanding and support to others, and to yourself.

Pause and check in. Take a moment to check in with yourself. How are you, really? Follow your breath in, and out. Notice how your body responds to the surface that supports you. Wiggle your fingers and toes. Ask your shoulders if they have room to drop. Follow another breath in, and out.

If you notice pain, offer a gentle hand to the place that is hurting. Let it know that you hear it. Sense how it is right now for the part in pain, from its point of view.

Acknowledge small losses. Take some time to acknowledge the small losses, the interruptions in routine and cancellations of eagerly anticipated events. These losses are no less real for being dwarfed by global events.

Sit with disappointment, and get a sense of exactly what you miss about your small losses. It might be fuzzy and unclear at first, and resolve into words or images as you spend time with it. Check if the words or images fit, or if there is more about that. Reflect back to yourself, *that* is what you miss. Sense how it is to have that heard.

When you feel ready, invite a sense of what might replace or approximate what you miss. Online connections instead of meeting in person. Local walks instead of more distant hikes. Broadcast recordings instead of missed concerts. The replacements are probably not as good, but they are better than nothing, and you can actively choose to find them.

Nurturing time. If one of your losses is bodywork appointments, you can take that hour as time for self-nurturing. It might feel good to lie down and invite your body to uncurl onto a supportive surface. Listen for what feels nurturing to you, and bring in as much of that as you can. You can add music, warmth, support under your knees, and a glass of water for when you get up. Give yourself a gentle transition into and out of your nurturing time.

Recognize your agency. All around the world, people are grieving small losses and finding alternatives. All around the world, people are grieving larger losses, perhaps shattered future plans or deaths of beloved friends and family.

All around the world, we are taking inventory of our skills and knowledge and generously sharing them with others. All around the world, we are choosing the stories we tell about this time. While acknowledging suffering and fear, we can turn toward generosity and gratitude and hope. Recognize your agency and your quiet heroism.

Adapt to New Risks

Agency gives you the power to choose which risks you lean into, and which you avoid. How do you relate to risks? Do you think of yourself as risk averse, risk tolerant, risk seeking, or some mixture? Is your approach different for physical, emotional, and financial risks?

Risk tolerance is affected by current resources. Can you recover from a bad outcome physically, emotionally, and financially? Do you have friends who cheer you on? Does your Inner Nurturer support you? Do you have an Inner Critic who yells about mistakes in an effort to keep you safe?

Nature and nurture. People seem to have a basic attitude toward risk built in from the start. Some small children charge forward, where others pause cautiously. When we experience risks that are matched to our abilities as we grow, we gain confidence in our choices.

As children, we learn not only about risk in general, but about the specific risks and dangers in our environment. Whether the dangers are being struck by a car, or being lost in the woods, or being shamed by a parent, we learn to recognize and manage them. We acquire strategies like "look both ways," or "carry a compass," or "never show vulnerability." Rigid global strategies like that last one limit us more than flexible localized strategies like the first two.

Ideally the adults around us teach us to evaluate risks, and support us when our choices do not turn out as we hoped. We absorb the ways they interact with risk in their lives.

When there is enough safety, we internalize that it is okay to be a clumsy beginner, and we can learn and improve our strategies through practice and play.

Worst outcomes. If we suffered abuse or other catastrophic experiences, and we were blamed in some way, it skews our perception of risk. "I did something, maybe I'm not even sure what, and the outcome was *that bad.*" We might become more risk averse to avoid more bad outcomes, or more risk seeking in an effort to gain mastery over the trauma.

Risks vary widely with our level of privilege and our individual circumstances. As Margaret Atwood said, "Men are afraid that women will laugh at them. Women are afraid that men will kill them." In the US, white people are afraid of property damage. Black people are afraid of being murdered by police.

New risks. When we move to a new job or a new neighborhood or a new country, our risks change in both subtle and obvious ways. We spend a lot of energy assessing the new environment and acquiring new strategies by trial and error, which is part of what makes change difficult. It takes time to adapt.

The Covid-19 pandemic has radically changed our risks, even when our surroundings have not changed. Suddenly we are coping with an invisible deadly threat and uncertain, changing information about it. We have to sift through conflicting news reports to piece together strategies that work for us.

Delayed feedback. Because the new coronavirus can be contagious before symptoms appear, and then it can take up to two weeks for the illness to become more severe, we do not receive prompt feedback to adjust our strategies. How do we protect others? How do we protect ourselves? Did we already have Covid-19? Tests are hard to get and false negatives are common*, so we keep wondering after having mild or moderate symptoms.

Conflicting cues. We naturally look to people around us for cues, subconsciously assuming that they must be more experienced, but this coronavirus is new for all of us at the same time. Our beliefs about the pandemic are affected by whom we trust both locally and at a distance as sources of accurate information.

The uncertainty and conflicting information are triggering for anyone who has been affected by gaslighting in the past. There is no consensus, so we see people around us with a wide range of strategies and evaluations of danger. Some wear masks, some do not. Some go about their lives as if nothing has changed. Some do not go out at all.

Some places are overwhelmed with cases, and some have very few. It can feel surreal to take the pandemic seriously when it is invisible. We worry about overreacting or under-reacting, "panic-mongering" or endangering people's lives, including our own. In addition to all the other struggles of an unprecedented world-wide pandemic, we feel shame at our inability to do it right.

Be a beginner. Allow yourself to be a beginner at handling this pandemic, or any new crisis. Pause, take a breath, and give yourself appreciation for all the discernments, decisions, and adjustments you have already made. Let yourself feel the nervousness of not knowing how to do it right, separately from all the other fears that may be there. Give the nervous part of yourself some kind attention and empathy.

---

* "What False Negatives Can Tell Us About Oregon's COVID-19 Numbers" by Erin Ross, May 26, 2020. https://opb.org/news/article/false-negative-coronavirus-test-oregon-deaths/

Beginners deserve space to go slowly, to mess up, and to get frustrated, as well as deserving guidance, reassurance, and celebration along the way. Bring in any positive memories you have of receiving support as a beginner, or of using your experience to support someone else.

Allow yourself to be affected by past trauma. Embrace the person you are in this moment, with your entire history of experiences, both positive and negative. Allow yourself to be reminded of other times you have been isolated, or crowded in with people you are not comfortable with, or struggled to get access to food. Notice what is the same and different to distinguish what happened then from what is happening now.

Focus on now. If you feel overwhelmed, narrow your focus to the thinnest slice of now, as Robyn Posin says. Let future-you handle future situations, and focus on what needs your attention in this moment. Perhaps you have already made all the decisions you currently need to make, and read all the news you currently need to read, and you can take a break.

Make room for your choices to be imperfect. You have limited, incomplete, possibly inaccurate information. You are doing the best you can with the resources you have. Let that be enough.

Risks of catching Covid-19. As of June 1, 2020, current understanding is that the major risk of catching Covid-19 is through inhaling air that a contagious person exhales* for more than 10-15 minutes. Talking, shouting, singing, coughing, and sneezing expel the breath with increasing force and

---

* "How Covid-19 Really Spreads" by Robert Roy Britt, May 27, 2020. https://elemental.medium.com/how-covid-19-really-spreads-f9627bb93645

therefore expel more viruses over a longer distance.

Unlike bacteria, viruses do not replicate outside the body. They might fall on a surface, but the concentration of live viruses decreases quickly over time. Touching a contaminated surface is a much smaller risk than inhaling contaminated air.

Covid-19 is a dangerous illness. While the risk of dying is relatively low for a young, healthy person, it is higher for older people and those with existing heart and lung issues. Covid-19 can also cause blood clots, strokes, and long-term debilitating fatigue* and lung damage.

For the sake of others, wear a mask whenever you leave the house. For your sake, avoid breathing inside air close to anyone not from your household as much as possible until we have a vaccine and/or effective treatment.

Conversations around risk. Take some time to notice your attitude toward risk in general, and then toward this pandemic. What risks, specifically, do you want to minimize? How do you evaluate your sources of information to make decisions? Who strongly influences you? Whom do you influence? Are there people you are regularly sharing air with? Have conversations with them about your perceptions and decisions around risk.

---

* "Long after the illness is gone, the damage from corona-virus may remain" by Peter Fimrite, May 31, 2020.
https://sfchronicle.com/health/article/Long-after-the-illness-is-gone-the-damage-from-15305842.php

Wear a Mask to Belong

When we choose our risks around Covid-19, we are choosing not just for ourselves, but for the family, friends, and strangers we associate with.

Many survivors of childhood abuse and neglect have an ongoing ache to belong, an unassuaged longing for the warmth of secure attachment. We develop strategies both to hide our vulnerable hearts and to reach out for connection. We hide our core self to be acceptable and we expose our rawness to be visible.

Belong right now. We think of belonging as something other people give or withhold from us, something we have to earn from them. We can choose to turn that around. We already belong as humans, as dwellers in a specific place, as descendants of specific people. We fundamentally belong because we exist as part of this earth.

Our heartbreak about not being loved the way we needed and deserved can coexist with the deep knowing that we belong right here, right now, in this body, in this place. No matter how temporary, precarious, unpleasant, or rejecting our surrounding circumstances are, we have a birthright of belonging already inside us.

Care for community. From that place of belonging and rootedness right here, right now, we have the honor and responsibility to care for our community: the land, animals, and people around us.

Care takes many forms in response to the needs of the

moment. In this time of global pandemic with the airborne virus* that causes Covid-19, there is one urgent action we can all take. Wear a mask or bandana. Cover your face every time you leave your home for any reason. Wear it over your nose and mouth, and for best protection, do not fuss with it once you have put it on.

Protect yourself and others. If you live in a place that took early, strong action to quell the virus completely, like New Zealand† or Mongolia‡, then look to your community to guide you on mask wearing. One reason those countries have been successful is that almost everyone acted together to protect their community. If you live in a place where the virus has subsided but is still quietly circulating, you are probably already wearing a mask. Keep it up!

If you live in a place where the virus is raging unchecked, like many states in the US, wear a mask for yourself and for others. Wear a mask in case you are breathing out viruses without knowing it. Wear a mask so that if someone else is breathing out viruses, you breathe in fewer and therefore get less ill that you would have if you were unmasked. Wear a mask even if you are only planning to be outside far away from others. You might run into a friend, or unexpectedly need to take public transit, or want to duck into a shop on the way home.

---

* "We Need to Talk About Ventilation" by Zeynep Tufekci July 30, 2020. https://theatlantic.com/health/archive/2020/07/why-arent-we-talking-more-about-airborne-transmission/614737/

† "Coronavirus: How New Zealand went 'hard and early' to beat Covid-19" by Anna Jones, BBC News, July 10, 2020. https://bbc.com/news/world-asia-53274085

‡ "COVID Underdogs: Mongolia" by Indi Samarajiva, May 18, 2020. https://medium.com/@indica/covid-underdogs-mongolia-3b0c162427c2

Wear a mask to instantly belong to the wider community of mask-wearers who care about the people around them.

Acknowledge resistance. There are a lot of reasons to resist wearing masks. They are uncomfortable, especially in the heat or while exercising. They fog our glasses. They make it harder to be heard when we speak. Unless they fit just right, they slide around and require adjustment, which is stressful when we want to avoid touching our face.

It might be triggering to have fabric against your face or to have your breathing even slightly impeded. You can name what is the same and different to distinguish what is triggered from the past from what is happening in the present. You can also try various mask designs to find one that works better for you.

Adaptable immigrants. We are all unwilling new immigrants to the Land of Covid-19, where we are separated from friends and loved ones, and everyday tasks like shopping have become unfamiliar and fraught with danger. Some of us come from neighboring lands of chronic illness and fragrance sensitivities where health issues had already imposed limitations on our lives.

If we do not already have the adaptive skills of an immigrant, we might try to cling to old ways instead of learning new ones. Putting on a mask every time we leave the house makes it forcefully real that our world has changed. We might imagine that if we ignore the problem of a worldwide pandemic, we can make it go away, especially if we already believe that positive thinking can control reality. It is important to allow the possibility of positive outcomes, and at the same time to acknowledge risks that are external to us.

Some of us live in local communities that express belonging by not wearing masks, joining together in resisting our new reality. Unfortunately, that requires balancing the risks of virus transmission with the risks of visibly expressing a difference from local practice. It can give a small taste of the experiences of people who move through the world with a difference of skin color, disability, gender expression, etc.

Continue social distancing. Adapting to change is hard. Living through a pandemic is hard. We can take it one day at a time while we do our best to protect ourselves and others.

Cloth masks reduce the risk of viral transmission while in unavoidable close proximity to others. Wearing a mask does not make it safe to spend extended periods of time breathing the same air with other people. We still need to practice social distancing. And it remains good hygiene to wash our hands often.

Even though physical masks make it harder to read expressions and connect with others in the ways we are used to, we can show warmth by nodding, waving, smiling (it shows in our eyes) and saying hello. We are already showing our respect and care by wearing a mask, and we can add to that with our words as needed.

Embrace all of yourself. When we feel the small aching lonely parts of us that want so terribly to belong, we can tend them by claiming them as parts of ourselves. They belong to us, with us. We can also warmly invite the parts of us that want nothing to do with those vulnerable parts. Those disdainful parts are ours too. We can embrace all of ourselves with the warmth and care we want from others.

Rock the Boat About Racism

Heartbreakingly, Covid-19 is infecting and killing a much higher percentage of BIPOC (Black, Indigenous, People of Color) than white people due to the inequities of past and present racism.*† Early in the pandemic, Black men were afraid to wear masks because their covered faces might be seen as more threatening.‡ In the US, the lack of universal healthcare and atrocious Covid-19 response are direct results of racism.

Notice your inner responses as you read about racism and white supremacy. Do you feel numb and bored? Do you feel angry and defensive? Do you feel relief because someone is naming your experience? When you pause with strong feelings and give them some space inside, you increase your capacity to acknowledge and disrupt racism.

---

* "Black People Are Dying From COVID-19 at Higher Rates Because Racism Is a Preexisting Condition" by Edwin Rios, Mother Jones, April 9, 2020. https://motherjones.com/coronavirus-updates/2020/04/black-people-are-dying-from-covid-19-at-higher-rates-because-racism-is-a-pre-existing-condition/

† "Covid-19's stunningly unequal death toll in America, in one chart" by Dylan Scott and Christina Animashaun, Vox, Oct 2, 2020. https://vox.com/coronavirus-covid19/2020/10/2/21496884/us-covid-19-deaths-by-race-black-white-americans

‡ "For Black Men, Fear That Masks Will Invite Racial Profiling" by Derrick Bryson Taylor, New York Times, April 14, 2020. https://nytimes.com/2020/04/14/us/coronavirus-masks-racism-african-americans.html

White supremacy thrives in the background, unseen and unacknowledged. It wants to be "the way things are," unnoticed, unquestioned, unresisted. While we associate white supremacy with Nazis and overt fascism, it is also the pernicious, pervasive idea that white people are more important and deserving than everyone else. Note that whiteness can be conditional, since light-skinned Jews are currently considered white, but can quickly become the targets of white supremacy.

We can resist white supremacy by seeing it and speaking about it. BIPOC parents teach their children to name and navigate racism that threatens their lives. White children have the privilege of remaining oblivious. Many white parents teach their children to avoid mentioning race in order not to "rock the boat."

We see the impact of white supremacy when white people are the ones promoted and elected to positions of power. We see it when white people are welcomed in stores while Black people are treated with suspicion. We see it when Black neighborhoods are first denied mortgages and then razed for freeways, ball parks, and hospitals, like Portland's Albina neighborhood.*

We see it in our books, TV shows, movies, and video games, where the viewpoint characters are white by default. Even if they are not, we often assume they are, especially when book covers are white-washed rather than showcasing characters with dark skin. In media, we see Black people depicted as villains, criminals, or support characters, rather than seeing them centered in their own lives.

---

* The Racist History of Portland, the Whitest City in America by Alana Semuels, The Atlantic, July 22, 2016. https://theatlantic.com/business/archive/2016/07/racist-history-portland/492035/

We see white supremacy inside us when it seems revolutionary to say that Black Lives Matter. In a just society, it would be obvious that every Black person's life is significant. Every Black person deserves protection, care, ease, and delight. No one deserves the ongoing trauma and destruction inflicted by racism.

There is potent shame pent up in the mechanics of white supremacy. Shame at the history of terrible acts, large and small, that have in stalled and maintained it. Shame at being numb to the suffering it requires. Shame at having an unfair advantage and not wanting to give it up. Shame at being made to feel less-than, and silenced about it.

The shame is passed down from adult to child, silencing questions and protests of unfairness. White people react wildly to being told something they said was racist, as if being called racist is worse than behaving in racist ways.

We can respond compassionately to that shame by thinking of it as white supremacy acting through us, rather than tainting us. Our goal is to help ourselves and others stop being unwitting channels for its evil.

Tolerate discomfort. Rhonda V. Magee, a Black professor of law at University of San Francisco, offers gentle mindfulness techniques to strengthen our capacity to tolerate shame and other uncomfortable emotions.* As we develop a practice of turning toward our emotions, we can let them flow through us rather than flood us, which gives us room to empathize with people around us.

BIPOC can use mindfulness to deflect the ongoing harm from microaggressions and choose how to respond. Magee recommends responding with kindness and empathy. Anger

---

* *The Inner Work of Racial Justice,* TarcherPerigee, 2019, by Rhonda V. Magee.

is also an option, even though white supremacy says it is not allowed. First bring compassion to the person being harmed, and then to the person causing harm.

A microaggression is a reminder about white supremacy, seemingly minor, but still hurtful, especially with repetition. Assuming a Black person on campus is a janitor rather than a professor. Asking a person with mixed ethnicity, "What *are* you?" Flinching away from a Black person in the elevator.

White people can start with willingness to be uncomfortable while learning about racism and becoming aware of internalized biased assumptions. Mindfulness creates a pause to prevent biases from spilling out to become microaggressions, or a pause for an apology afterward.

For example, a person of mixed race might respond angrily to being asked where they are from, because they get asked all the time and they have lived here all their life. A mindful pause allows the person who asked to respond with empathy rather than defensiveness.

Personal affirmative action. When white people do favors and extend help to other white people by unconscious default, BIPOC continue to be at a disadvantage. White people can commit to personal affirmative action and make a conscious effort to be kind to people with less privilege, not as a rescuer, but as a fellow human being.

Talk about racism. While Black people have to talk about racism to navigate daily life, white people generally avoid the topic. Perhaps you already discuss racism with like-minded people. When protests are in the news, perhaps you remind people that lives are more important than property.

As a white person, whatever your current level of engagement, think about how you can take one more step. Mention anti-racist books and articles you are reading. Ask others what they are learning. Use the communication skills you already have to listen and understand others' viewpoints and share yours.

Be mindful around your sense of danger while discussing racism. Test it out with small risks. Notice white supremacy in action, warning you to stay quiet to keep its benefits. Notice when your words are well-received. Notice when you are encountering a wall.

While taking one step past your usual comfort zone, do not abandon your sense of what is too much for you. You can withdraw from conversations that become cruel or overwhelming and return to the topic another day. Talking about racism is a skill that develops over time.

Look back kindly. As you learn more about anti-racism, look back kindly on your past self. When past missteps come to mind, breathe through the shame of having behaved in racist ways, and be glad you are learning and growing. Bring that open-hearted kindness to the people around you as well.

White supremacy is a catastrophe for everyone. While BIPOC are affected more directly and urgently, the numbness and disconnection of white supremacy are terrible for white people too. The collective disaster of climate change is made worse by white supremacy's callous lack of care for people of color.

White people: for yourself and for all of us, gently gather your courage, step forward, and talk about racism.

How to Resist Enough

We want to be good people. For ourselves and for the world around us, we urgently want to *do something* about white supremacy, rising fascism, climate change, and other ongoing disasters, but it never seems like enough.

How do we resist enough? How do we know that we are speaking up enough and doing our part, whether our side is losing or winning? How do we choose our priorities between the big picture and the small details of our lives? How do we care for ourselves and each other amid ongoing authoritarian threats to our political infrastructure?

In part, these are spiritual questions that we each have to answer for ourselves. What effect do we want to have on the world? What is our role to play? What is the right way to live for each of us? What qualities do we admire in good people?

Sustainable resistance. When the news is overwhelming and triggering, we leap into the urgency and panic of Emergency Mode. We burn our resources at an unsustainable rate, borrowing from the future because emergencies are supposed to be short-term. The stream of bad news shows no signs of stopping. We need to change our strategies and our standards to integrate resistance sustainably into our lives.

A key part of sustainable resistance is allowing ourselves to feel how we feel, whether it is guilt, horror, rage, fear, or joy. All our emotions and reactions are valid.

When the bad news is happening to you—fire, or deportation, or hate crimes, or losing vital medical care—then it makes sense to be in Emergency Mode. Your resistance can be to reach out to others for help and support.

Resistance can be affirmative, creative, connected, nourishing. When we say No to one thing, what are we saying Yes to? How can we make our Yeses louder? When our resistance helps us live the way we want to live, we are succeeding even if the specific cause or battle is lost.

Balanced resources. To be sustainable, our resistance has to use fewer personal resources than we take in overall. Some resources are easy to inventory, like free time and money. Some are harder, like energy and resilience. We can monitor our resources over time, and notice if we are feeling drained or desperate. We can choose resistance that supports and nourishes us at the same time as making a difference in the world.

We each carry a mix of privilege and oppression, comfort and strain. If we already live in Emergency Mode because of past or ongoing trauma, our resistance might start with learning new skills of self-care and living within our limits in sustainable ways. If we lead a busy modern life but have resources to spare, we can spend more time, energy, or money on resistance and keep an eye on our ongoing resource balance.

Many ways to resist. We might believe that resistance only looks one way, and that it has to be all or nothing. In truth, every little bit counts. We can focus on a few issues that matter most to us. We each do the piece we are currently called to do, in a way that fits our resources, skills and aptitudes. We have to trust that others around us are doing their part. No one can carry the weight of the world alone.

Resistance includes:
- Creating and leading organizations

- Creating and leading events
- Attending meetings and events
- Spreading the word about meetings and events
- Donating to organizations and organizers
- Creating art and writing that expresses resistance
- Buying art and writing
- Emotional and logistical support for resistance
- Naming oppression out loud in our daily lives
- Shopping locally and being mindful of what our spending supports
- Doing our inner work
- All the ways to make the world a better place

Resist with your strengths. As we consider adding resistance activities, we can take into account our strengths and skills, and what we want more or less of in our lives. For some people, calling political representatives is easy. For some it is hard, but doable. For some it is terrifying. We do not need more terror in our lives.

Some people want more connection and might want to join a group or lead one. Some people have social anxiety and would prefer to do activism online or by sending money.

Some want to do more service and can contribute volunteer hours and emotional labor toward resistance. Some are already overwhelmed with service for jobs and families and need some space where no one is adding more demands.

Some can contribute small monthly donations or larger one-time donations. Seek out local organizations as well as ones that are nationally known.

Join with skilled people. We are not resisting alone. Organized resistance is a set of skills that many people have already practiced. For example, BIPOC have been living with oppression and discrimination for far too long, and many have learned how to resist both politically and personally. If we cannot find an existing organization, we can form a group of people who want to learn together.

Randy Blazak, Chair of Oregon's Coalition Against Hate Crimes, said that resistance against racism can be divided into institutional, community, and personal activism.* We can divide all kinds of resistance into those three categories.

Institutional resistance – please vote. Resistance at the institutional level changes laws, runs for office, calls elected representatives, signs petitions, and votes. Please vote in every election, including the ones with only local issues or candidates on the ballot. Local politics directly affects you and your neighbors.

If you want to call your representatives, 5calls.org makes it easy to know who to call and what to say about currently important issues.

Community resistance. Resistance at the community level goes to protests, gets out the vote, runs meetings, teaches others about resistance, and intervenes when someone is being bullied.

Personal resistance. Resistance at the personal level learns about privilege and oppression and builds daily self-awareness about how we participate in those systems. Personal resistance is also self-care, unpacking the ways we believe we are not enough, and treating ourselves with compassion. When we work to heal ourselves, we reduce the harm that trauma and abuse do in the world, both because we deserve to feel better, and because we learn to treat others better.

---

* "White America: Become an Ally through Education & Dismantle Racism," panel discussion with Randy Blazak at RaceTalks, October 10, 2017. https://racetalkspdx.com

Wider perspectives. As we read books by women, people of color, and other marginalized groups, we learn about other perspectives. We gradually learn to question the pervasive centering of straight cis white men in our narratives and in our lives. It is an ongoing practice to decenter the ways we are privileged and listen to those with less privilege.*

There are classes about resisting oppression and workshops on how to intervene in bigotry or hate crimes. Search online for classes and bystander intervention trainings local to you.†

Adjust over time. When you feel overwhelmed, desperate, or worn out, give yourself kind permission to pull back rather than push forward. Perhaps you can reduce the amount of news you take in. Notice which activities nourish you, and which drain you. Your life and your well-being matter. Resist by seeking support.

You are enough. Working toward what you believe in is a lifelong practice. The specifics will change over time. Give yourself credit for the choices you have already built into your life, like recycling or reduced car use. Remember that you are not alone, and that you are doing what you can. If you doubt that you are doing enough, resist more in some way. If you get overwhelmed, resist less. Kindness to yourself and others is also resistance.

---

* See "Resources" on page 70 for a starting reading list.

† "Bystander Intervention Training" from Hollaback! against harassment and abuse.
https://ihollaback.org/resources/bystander-resources/

Mend What You Can Reach

"The growing good of the world is partly dependent on unhistoric acts; and that things are not so ill with you and me as they might have been, is half owing to the number who lived faithfully a hidden life, and rest in unvisited tombs." —George Eliot, Middlemarch

As we find ways to resist what is wrong in the world, we can reduce the strain on our nervous systems by taking charge of our exposure to news and by finding ways to take positive action locally.

Limit exposure. For many of us, bad news can jump out at us any time. Sound bites on TV, broadcasts on the car radio, news feeds in the browser, alerts on our phones or watches. When we turn off all the ways news automatically reaches us, we can make choices about how much news we consume, and in what formats.

There are terrible events happening in the world, and at the same time many people are peacefully going about their lives. Most news broadcasts are designed to scare us and keep us on the edge of our seats for the next update. To interrupt that cycle of urgency, we can choose a time to catch up on the main headlines and stop looking when we feel overwhelmed. If something big and important happens, people around us will let us know.

We can seek positive news stories and ask people to share their good news. We can actively build hopeful narratives to replace the story that everything is doomed.

Local action. When we reduce our exposure to panic-inducing news, we free up time and energy for other aspects of our lives, including pitching in to help within our reach. No matter how small, mundane, quirky, or seemingly irrelevant, everyone's contribution helps make the world a better place.

When we each pick up litter near our homes, we can collectively enjoy a cleaner streetscape. We naturally try to improve local conditions when we feel a sense of community, tribe, or kinship. Even when we feel isolated, we can choose to take more care, and perhaps find a sense of community along the way.

What is within reach varies for each person, physically, emotionally, and mentally. Sometimes our reach is bigger than we imagine. Sometimes our reach is smaller than we demand from ourselves.

Already contributing. Start by giving yourself credit for what you are already doing. Did you grow up in an abusive family? Are you pouring time and energy into healing so that you can stop the cycle of abuse and interact in more positive ways? Each person who turns away from abusive patterns contributes to the overall health of the world. Your healing ripples out to help everyone you interact with.

Do you run a hobby group or tend a garden or post to a blog about your little corner of expertise? Do you cook meals and keep order at home? Do you show up for friends in crisis? Your care contributes to the weave of everyday life for yourself and those who depend on you.

Do you reuse bags and recycle and save energy where you can? Do you take the bus or ride a bike or carpool? As we each turn toward living more sustainably, we add our weight to the tipping point where sustainability is the default. Even though individual actions cannot solve our climate crisis, we can all work to generate less plastic trash and live more lightly on the earth.

We each live more sustainably in some ways and less sustainably in others depending on our needs, capabilities, and situations. If your Inner Critic constantly harps on everything you are doing wrong, let it know that you hear it, and check if perhaps it is worried.

Mend objects. When we mend what is within our reach, we improve our world and reduce what we need to discard.

Mending of all sorts takes time, skill, tools, and often money as well. We each have different realms where we already know how to mend or want to learn, and realms where it is too overwhelming or out of our reach. Mending also requires discernment about when something is beyond repair, or not worth the effort for us.

We could physically mend our clothing, our shoes, our tools, and our devices, or pay someone with the expertise to do so. If it is within our budget, we can purchase sturdier items that are repairable rather than disposable.

Mend relationships. We could emotionally mend our relationships, asking questions before lashing out, and expressing boundaries before assuming bad intent. If we need to walk away, we could do it with a minimum of harm.

We could mend our frayed selves, allowing ourselves more rest and nourishment. We could make a practice of appreciating our efforts and improvements. We could notice what does not work in our lives, and make small or large changes toward more ease.

Make grace. We could make room to be the agent of grace for others.

- Return a lost item anonymously.
- Donate unneeded treasures for others to delight in finding.
- Give people (including ourselves) slack for reacting out of anxiety or shame, while still expecting respectful treatment.
- Work to use non-oppressive language and treat people with kindness.
- Give positive feedback. Tell people that you see and appreciate their quiet work of mending.

While we cannot fix every looming issue, we might be able to help with one of them. We could take on or join a larger project to mend injustice, solve a problem, or create joy. Our particular combination of skills and interests might make a bigger difference than we expect. For example, C. Todd Kennedy collects and farms rare fruit trees.* He has saved roughly half of the US's stone fruit varieties.

Action sparks hope. When we take small actions within our reach, we restore our sense of being able to affect our world in difficult times. Not only do we contribute to general improvement for everyone, we also restore our own hope and well-being.

---

* "The Quiet Rescue of America's Forgotten Fruit" by Anne Ewbank, March 27, 2018, Atlas Obscura. https://atlasobscura.com/articles/growing-collecting-rare-fruit

Resources

The Inner Work of Racial Justice, TarcherPerigee, 2019, by Rhonda V. Magee gently helps you build the skills to tolerate strong emotions around anti-racism.

Me and White Supremacy, Sourcebooks, 2020, by Layla Saad brilliantly breaks white supremacy into its components and asks white people to step up to change it.

"The Election, Lao Tzu, a Cup of Water" by Ursula K. Le Guin talks about studying peace. "The election of 2016 was one of the battles of the American Civil War." https://bookviewcafe.com/blog/2016/11/21/the-election-lao-tzu-a-cup-of-water/

"An Anarchist Quaker's Prayer to Soothe Anxiety" by Ayu Sutriasa's therapist encourages us to put down the world's anguish for a moment. https://yesmagazine.org/opinion/2020/03/24/coronavirus-prayer-anxiety/

A safety plan is a personalized, practical plan to improve your safety while experiencing abuse, preparing to leave an abusive situation, or after you leave. Checklists and resources: https://calltosafety.org/services/safety-planning/

All the links in this book are clickable at:
https://traumahealed.com/embodying-hope-links/

3: Uncomfortable Emotions

It makes sense to have huge uncomfortable emotions in response to huge uncomfortable events. A big part of healing from trauma is learning to manage overwhelming emotions from the past. Fortunately, those skills transfer to emotions in the present.

Our emotions are signals about what is true for our bodies. Pushing them away or numbing them saves them for later, perhaps to reemerge as PTSD. When we can experience our emotions, allowing them to flow through us without flooding us, it frees us to stay in the present moment.

We receive messages that we "should" keep our emotions small and contained and convenient for others so we stay pleasant and productive. While it can be more enjoyable to feel calm and settled, it is sometimes more authentic to be furious or terrified or grief-stricken.

We can grow our capacity to handle big emotions with

Embodying Hope

practice and support. Our sturdy, resilient adult self can turn toward everything inside us with compassion, including the parts that hate the emotions we are experiencing.

It can feel vulnerable to allow our emotions to fill us all the way to our edges rather than hiding them away inside. When other people can sense our emotions and resonate with them, we feel less lonely and more accompanied.

Powerful emotions can move us to powerful actions. When we embody all our emotions, we can embody hope as well.

Counter the Feelings Police

When my friend tells me about her cancer diagnosis, I ask what I can do to help. I know about Susan Silk's ring theory for crises.* You draw a bunch of concentric circles with the person in crisis at the center, people closest to them in the next ring, and less close people in outer rings. The rule is, "Comfort IN, dump OUT." Ask for support from someone less affected by the crisis.

The ring theory does not say, "People in outer rings don't get to have feelings," nor, "These are the feelings and intensity required at each ring." Our emotional responses are messages about what we sense and how it affects us, uniquely tied in with our individual history and personality. Someone in an inner ring might be stoic and calm. Someone in an outer ring might weep uncontrollably.

Trying to keep order. We absorb the idea that there is a right way to feel, and a right length of time to feel that way. There is a push from society to remain productive and not inconvenience anyone else unduly. People close to us might be uncomfortable with strong emotions and want to avoid feeling helpless.

There is also a push from inside to avoid feeling overwhelmed. We develop an internal Feelings Police both as a defense against people policing our feelings from the outside,

---

* "How not to say the wrong thing" by Susan Silk and Barry Goldman, April 7, 2013. https://articles.latimes.com/2013/apr/07/opinion/la-oe-0407-silk-ring-theory-20130407

and because we lack the tools to manage our emotions. The internal Feelings Police is genuinely trying to keep order, which is useful in a true emergency when you need to act first and feel later. Unfortunately, they often forget to stand down when the emergency is over.

Sense your Feelings Police. What do you notice about your inner Feelings Police? Are they a faint whisper, or one voice among many, or are they in charge?

What tools do they use to keep your feelings squashed? They might use shame, for example, "Big boys/girls don't cry." They might use dissociation, so you feel calm in a spacy, vague way. They might say others are more important, and you do not deserve to take up space with your feelings. They might say your feelings are wrong, or bad, or too much, or too little, or too conflicted. You can let these critical voices know that you hear them, and they get to feel exactly the way they feel for as long as that's so.

Sensitivity is fine. Both external and internal Feelings Police love to say, "You're too sensitive." As Robyn Posin writes*, we can translate that as, "More sensitive than they are comfortable with," and reflect it back as a neutral statement. "I hear that I seem too sensitive to you." No defense of sensitivity is required, because there is nothing wrong with sensitivity. To a friend, or an inner voice, we could add, "Maybe you can share what you are worried about."

People who are prevented from listening to their feelings are easier to derail, control, and gaslight. Criticism of emotions can be part of a Tone Argument used to silence someone with less power. "You sound angry, so I can ignore you." Abusers do not want their victims to realize that they are

---

* "Being Too Much" by Robyn Posin.
http://forthelittleonesinside.com/being-too-much

feeling terrible because of the abuse, not because of innate flaws. Emotions can motivate and fuel change.

Anchor in the present. Our emotional responses are a mix of past and present, internal cues and external stimuli. They are a shining ribbon of information about what is true for us. When we can witness our emotions without being swept away by them, they keep us anchored in the present. "Right now, I feel angry. Right now I feel happy. Right now I feel confused and uncertain about what I feel." Since emotions are physical responses in the body, we can also name physical sensations: clenched jaw, pulled-in shoulders, headache, upset stomach, or on the positive side, open shoulders, head high, free breathing.

Our emotions might not feel the way we expect. For example, grief might be silent and immobile with shock, like the first moment after a fall. It might feel like physical pain, or like a bottomless ocean. It might want to curl up small, or to run around and organize everything. It might come and go unpredictably, or not show up at all, with no regard for "appropriate" schedules. It might snag on ungrieved losses that seemed unimportant at the time.

Happily, I hear that my friend's cancer is treatable. The Feelings Police pop up about good news, too. How much am I allowed to celebrate? What about people who are not hearing good news right now? I can allow both relief about her reprieve and sadness about her illness to move through me.

Make room for feelings. We can intentionally make room for all our feelings when they feel chaotic and overwhelming. Paradoxically, spending a little time to give them more space tends to make them more manageable, even if nothing else changes.

- Start with the sensation or emotion on the surface. It

might be confusion, a sense of overwhelm, a named emotion, a desire for things to be different, or a physical sensation.
- Offer that first layer a specific spot in the room and see if it is willing to move over there for a while. You might get a sense of its size, texture, color, or other qualities.
- If it is not willing to move away, check if you can get as much distance as a piece of paper between you and it. If it is still unwilling, you could sense if you can give it more space inside you. You can also shift focus to the unwillingness and offer it some room.
- Sense how it feels to have a little more space inside.
- As new emotions and sensations surface, continue to give each a spot in the room and sense a bit about it.
- When nothing more comes, take a few breaths and enjoy the spaciousness of being exactly how you are in this moment.

If you are keeping a friend company when they are having big feelings, you can make room for them in the same way. You do not have to fix or change anything. Let your friend know you hear them, and their feelings make sense, and they get to feel the way they do for as long as that's so. When you can allow your big feelings, it becomes easier to allow someone else to have them too.

Emotions flow and change. Emotions are meant to move. Giving them more space allows them to flow and change, peak and ebb. As we become more comfortable with giving them space, our Feelings Police can quiet down and rest.

Depression: Natural Response to Trauma

When the Feelings Police successfully push down our spontaneous responses, we might feel depressed. A heavy reluctance to get up in the morning. A weight presses down all day, makes it hard to move, squeezes the joy out of everything. Voices inside say, "Worthless. Shameful. Failure." Tears, sadness, grief, despair. Emptiness. Hopelessness.

A common narrative says that depression is caused by a malfunction of the body and brain, leading to symptoms of ongoing sadness, lack of enjoyment, disturbed sleep, disturbed eating habits, and possibly suicidal thoughts and actions. That narrative fits some people's depression that comes and goes independent of external circumstances and is kept at bay with medications.

Symptoms of loss. Depression can also be a natural response to past or present circumstances, not a malfunction at all. Psychologists acknowledge that symptoms of depression largely overlap with symptoms of grief and bereavement. When we experience a big loss or life change, we need time to mourn and adapt. The body's response says, "This loss matters. This was part of me."

Young children fall into depression when they are separated from their parents or other attachment figures for too long. Adults and children alike need to know that we are important to people around us and we can depend on them. We need people who delight in us when things are going well and comfort us when we are in pain.

Pushing something down. Depression can also come from using a lot of our energy to push down (depress) something. Depression could be anger turned inward because it is unsafe to express it toward an external target. Depression could be about dead-end jobs and fear of the future as it keeps getting harder to afford housing and food and healthcare for large numbers of people.

Trauma increases all these reasons for depression. It involves loss of safety, and usually other losses. It leads to isolation. And it causes overwhelming emotions that have to be pushed down to allow day-to-day functioning.

Isolation and trauma. Isolation is both a cause and consequence of trauma. During and after a traumatic event, our nervous system returns to balance more quickly if there are other supportive nervous systems around, since nervous systems entrain or synchronize with each other. In times of stress, our bodies especially like to be close to the people we are attached to, but any kind presence helps us feel soothed and safe.

If we go through traumatic events alone and unsupported, we are stuck with the overwhelming feelings left behind. This is especially hard for babies and young children. Their undeveloped nervous systems need calming adult nervous systems nearby to help them manage big emotions and overwhelming events.

Past trauma can also lead to isolation. When our nervous system is already dysregulated, it is harder to establish and maintain friendships. PTSD symptoms such as anxiety and flashbacks get in the way of light conversation. People might not want to hear about the realities of trauma, either because they have been lucky enough to avoid it, or because it brings up their own history in a way they cannot manage.

Need for belonging. Belonging is a basic need. Isolation can bring up painful feelings of shame and not being normal enough. We might work very hard at healing in order to acquire enough skills to belong, and then ironically find that our skills at naming the truth of our experiences make it harder to fit in with others. We try to solve the problem of belonging individually by fixing ourselves, but it is a cultural, societal problem.

Pandemic-related isolation has made the negative effects more widely understood, but also intensified the problems for people who were already isolated.

Depression is a natural consequence of isolation. Bereft of support and positive connection, we fold in on ourselves and start to wonder why we work so hard to function in this world.

Suicidal thoughts. Thoughts of self-harm and suicide are often part of depression. An inner voice says, seemingly at random, "I want to die," or "I should kill myself." Visions of falls, car crashes, or other catastrophes float up unbidden. Secret envy arises when someone dies suddenly.

If you have a plan to kill yourself, please read "Thinking About Suicide? Read This First" at metanoia.org/suicide/. Reach out for help! Call a suicide hotline such as 1-800-SUICIDE, or your local emergency services at 911. You deserve help, and you deserve to live.

Suicidal feelings can be ongoing without a plan to act on them. When an inner voice wants to die, it has a reason. There might be overwhelming physical and emotional pain, intense shame, current or past helplessness, or flashbacks to freeze during trauma. You can listen for what triggers or surrounds that inner voice, and keep it company.

Hidden critic. The despondent inner voice might be responding to messages from an underground Inner Critic who sows shame in a misguided attempt to be safer from attacks from the outside world. Barbara McGavin writes about "checking the undergrowth" when she notices feelings of shame and despair. She recommends turning toward both the collapsing part and attacking part with kind attention. "They need to be heard, sensed, allowed to say just how bad it is, and just exactly how it is that bad for them."*

Inner parts that want to die might be caught in flashbacks to earlier times when it looked like dying was the only way out from abusive situations. Even if life is still hard now, it is important to take note of our increased resources and options as adults.

Increased options. The inertia of depression can make it hard to take advantage of our increased options. When energy is limited and everything looks hopeless, it is hard to know what changes might make things better. Look for opportunities in small glimmerings of hope, a slight lift of interest in trying something new, or a slight increase in energy.

When you can, make small changes. Look for patterns in when you feel better and worse. Pay attention to the things you have "always known" you need. Gradually, you will find strategies that help consistently.

Look at physical reasons for depression. Vitamin deficiencies and food intolerances can drastically affect energy and

---

* Barbara McGavin, "The 'Victim', the 'Critic' and the Inner Relationship: Focusing with the Part that Wants to Die."
https://focusingresources.com/the-victim-the-critic-and-the-inner-relationship-focusing-with-the-part-that-wants-to-die/

mood. If you have access to a doctor or naturopath, get a physical checkup. Try spending more time outside, or find indoor movement you like, such as yoga. In the depths of winter, consider using a light box.

When you can afford the risk of rejection, reach out for support. To counter ongoing isolation, notice and treasure even brief connections. To connect with yourself, try meditation, a chance to simply pay attention to what is true for you right now.

Determination to live. Being alive is supposed to feel good. Basic bodily functions like movement, eating, breathing, sleeping, and connection with other beings are meant to be intrinsically rewarding. When trauma disconnects us from our bodies, we disconnect from that spark of joy.

Sense inside for your tenacious determination to live, the force that keeps you reaching out for help and reading articles and continuing to trudge forward even when you feel terrible.

Not broken. I prefer a narrative with hope about depression. You are not broken. Your responses make sense. As you find ways to sit with inner terror and misery and loneliness for as long as they are there, they will gradually shift and make room for new feelings.

Anchor Terror in Time

Terror is part of the body's basic survival mechanisms. It says, "I sense something that threatens my life, and I want to live!" As unpleasant as it feels, terror is not an enemy in itself. It is a blaring alarm.

There are so many reasons to feel terror these days. Each threat affects our nervous systems differently. The pandemic virus is invisible and we receive conflicting information about the right actions to take. In contrast, the burning smell and eerie reddish light from wildfires awaken a primal need to flee. Militarized police impose an ever-present dread of random violence on Black lives. Crumbling political institutions bring a slow-motion threat of a constricted future.

Check in. As you continue to read about terror, and any time there is no immediate emergency, invite yourself to slow down. Pause to check in with your body, and take breaks as needed.

When you feel terror (extreme fear) or panic (extreme anxiety):
- Breathe
- Evaluate
- Act
- Connect
- Soothe past terror
- Plan for the future

Breathe. When your system is flooded with terror, bring

your attention to your breath. Simply notice that you are still breathing. Invite your in-breath to bring in a little more air. Invite your out-breath to be a little longer than your in-breath. Note: forcing your breathing to change can add more distress. Be gentle. Does your body want to make sound, a whine or whimper or yell?

Evaluate. Name your sensations to yourself. Rapid heartbeat, tingling face, staring eyes, clenched shoulders, breathlessness, agitation. The urge to flee, or back into a defensible corner, or lash out. The urge to find and cling to someone you love.

Look around at your current situation. Name what you observe. Is there imminent physical danger, like visible flames? Is there a current emergency, like evacuation orders?

Offer calm company for the terror by saying, "I sense a part of me that is terrified." Feel your present-time adult body, your size and strength and capabilities.

Act. When there is a present-time emergency, channel terror into action. As much as terror might scream at you to do everything at once, it works better to give attention to one task at a time.

If your system goes into freeze, keep noticing your body and your surroundings until movement feels possible again. Bring in as much kind acceptance as you can, including for the part that is yelling about being immobile. In every moment, your system is doing its very best to keep you alive.

Connect. Terrified bodies often want other bodies nearby for soothing and support. When my cat was terrified by a vet visit, she pressed herself against my belly for comfort and protection. Reach out to trusted people or pets for physical contact if they are available to you. Strangers can quickly become calming support in an emergency. Next best is phone, video, or text/email with someone you trust.

If you cannot reach for a personal connection, search online for stories from people who have been in similar situations. No matter how alone you feel, you are not the first or only person to go through your situation.

Soothe past terror. After dealing with any imminent threats, you can bring kind attention to soothing past terror. If your emotions are out of scale with current events, it might be an emotional flashback or a flashback to a time before you had language.

Your adult self can offer comfort and reassurance to the terrified inner child. Anchor yourself in present sensations and the certainty that whatever the past terrifying situation was, it did end and you did survive. Put a gentle hand over your belly or heart if that feels comforting.

Be kind to your terrified body. Seek out comfort, warmth, and containment. Wrap up in a blanket, perhaps a weighted blanket. Wear soft, comfortable clothes. Hold a cup of tea. Cuddle a stuffed animal or pillow. Eat something calming. Listen to soothing familiar music.

Plan for the future. Are you terrified about the future? Pull in the perimeter of your attention to a manageable time horizon, perhaps five minutes, or a few days. Anchor yourself in the immediate present. You might be right that the future will be terrible, and it is not happening yet.

Acknowledge terror's signal, "This will be bad! Do something!" Seek out information from multiple sources and build an internal sense of what might happen. Plan as best you can for bad outcomes, and take action toward the future you want to see.

Let it move. Terror is a natural part of being alive. Let it breathe, move, cry, scream. Afterwards, your system will settle toward calm. Continue to limit your perimeter of attention to the immediate present when you start to feel overwhelmed. You might notice that you have been living with a background of terror for a while.

You might find a sense of containment and reassurance in physical movement, a walk or run or bike ride. If you cannot fix the large problems, fix small ones and create order in your living space. Get out your mending pile. Organize your junk drawer. Pull some weeds in the garden.

Conditions that are new and terrifying for some of us are familiar for others. Hazardous air quality from wildfire smoke is a shock for many of us on the west coast of the US, but old news for people living downwind from industrial pollutants. As we adapt to unfamiliar hazards, we can also use our new understanding to push for improved conditions for everyone suffering those hazards. Mend what you can reach.

Trust your resilience. Terror moves us to act in the present, shows us where kind attention is needed to heal our past, and directs us to prepare for the future. Listen to its messages, and trust that future-you will be able to handle future conditions, just as you are now handling the demands of the present. Notice the resources and resilience you have already gathered to help you adapt to difficult situations and events.

Lift the Anger Lid With Care

Like terror, anger is part of our basic survival mechanisms. It gives us important information about how our environment affects us and what we want to be different.

When you get angry, does an internal lid clamp down, perhaps before you even notice you are angry? Or does your anger spill out in a way that feels overwhelming, making you wish for a lid? You may have absorbed beliefs early on that your anger was bad, or that anger is always abusive, or that only certain powerful people are allowed to be angry.

A part of you might be worried that your anger will hurt those around you, or that others will dismiss or punish you for being angry, or that anger is "negative" and will hurt you with its presence.

In fact, anger is energy moving in the body, a natural part of being alive. Even when people around us disapprove, we can turn toward and acknowledge our anger. Depending on the situation, we can choose to express it in a non-abusive way.

Covering cascade. When we believe our anger is not acceptable, a lightning-quick cascade covers it with sadness, numbness, self-criticism, or distraction. It might feel suddenly urgent to eat something, go for a run, say a few affirmations, or otherwise soothe the anger back into quiescence. The cascade might end in fuzzy dissociation, jittery anxiety, or heavy depression, leaving us wondering what just happened and why we feel so bad.

Anger says, "I am here, I matter, and I don't like that." "That" might be urgent and personal, for example someone violating a boundary, or it might be more distant or global. We might respond with anger to a memory of a violation, or to seeing someone else be hurt, or to larger wrongs like the destruction of the environment or the mishandling of a pandemic or the ongoing murders and maltreatment of Black people.

Reacting parts. We can frame the cascade as a series of parts, each reacting in turn. You might be aware of two parts:
- Something in me is angry
- *And* something in me puts a lid on it (or wishes it could).

You might notice additional steps in your cascade:
- *And* something in me finds a distraction
- *And* something in me feels ashamed
- *And* something in me feels hopeless about the whole thing.*

Caringly turn toward. When we include these parts in our larger awareness and caringly turn toward each one in turn, we can help them connect with our present-time resources. Over time, rather than each part trying desperately to solve the problem in their narrow section of the cascade, we feel big and flexible enough to contain and address our initial anger as a whole.

The cascade starts because a part of us believes that it is not safe to assert that we are here, that we matter, and that we do not like something. We can invite the part that holds that belief into our awareness, and sense what happens when it

---

* Phrasing suggested by Ann Weiser Cornell and Barbara McGavin as part of Untangling®.

is activated by the beginning of anger. When you make that invitation, what do you feel in your body?

Constraining lid. Angry energy is often expressed with a loud voice and expansive movements. Anger takes up space. The effort to constrain anger often pulls your body down and in, keeping you small, quiet, unobtrusive. As you pay attention to the constraining part, you might sense a web of tension through your chest, shoulders, neck, and jaw.

Keep it company. Bring in a gentle breath to meet that tension. Let it know that you are there, keeping it company. You might sense relief from a young part trying to manage situations that are far too much for it. The part might show you a series of memories when it has worked hard to keep you safe. Let it know you hear each one, and acknowledge how hard it has been working.

You might also hear about present-time reasons to stay small and unnoticed. Everyone deserves safe space to feel anger, and you know best what is safe for you in an abusive situation.

Listen to shame. Constrained anger often turns inward as shame, self-criticism, or self-harm. Do you notice a part who tells you how bad you are for being angry, and a part who believes it? Self-harm might include skin-picking, cutting, unnecessary risks, and other punishments. You can invite the punishing part to chat with the larger you who contains all these parts. You might sense for what it is trying to protect you from, and underneath that, what it wants for you. The goal is to listen deeply, until that part feels met and understood.

You can also sense into the part who feels punished, keep it company, and listen deeply for what it wants and does not want for all of you. You might notice that underneath their conflict, both parts are doing their best to find safety and survival. Take time to sense how it feels to be the larger witness self accompanying them both.

Receive old shock. As you sit with them, you might notice an underlying fear or shock. When you listen patiently, the fearful part might show you one or more original moments when small you expressed anger with a loud voice and flailing movements, and a violent, cruel, or abandoning response stuffed the anger right back down into your body.

Let this young one know that you hear them. Provide a warm pool of care and compassion to receive the old shock and fear that had nowhere to go back then. Give them plenty of time to take in this new safety. As they relax, you might sense changes in your body where you had not been aware of holding tight until it starts to let go.

Greet anger. When you feel ready, invite the angry part into your awareness. What do you sense in your body? Can you sense more about the specific flavor and intensity of anger? It might be aggravated, irked, livid, or irate.* A combination of words, images, gestures, and sensations might convey how this particular anger feels right now.

You might ask this part to tell you more about what has stirred the anger. Whether it is past or present, large or small, the response is valid and gets to be there for as long as it is there. As you make a warm, kind space around this angry part, keep sensing whether it feels heard. Does anything change in your body as you sit with it?

Fuel for change. As you get to know the various parts of your cascade, you can recognize their presence in your body.

---

* The Nonviolent Communication Feelings Inventory has many words for anger and other feelings.
https://cnvc.org/training/resource/feelings-inventory

You will start to notice them while they do their work, rather than afterwards. With time, you will sense your anger and be able to choose how to respond to it with all your present-time resources.

You are here. You matter. Make space for your anger and thank it for letting you know something is happening that you do not like. Anger can fuel change toward more kindness, more truth, more respect, and more justice.

Sit with Disappointment

Sometimes anger arises out of disappointment. The hardware store is out of the item we need. A friend did not show up when they said they would. The job went to someone else. The election went to the other candidate.

Disappointments come in all shapes and sizes. How we handle them depends on our expectations, our inner resources and resilience at the time, our external resources to work around the problem, and the story we tell ourselves.

Early lessons. What did your parents and other adults teach you about disappointment? Did they name it and make room for it? "I see that you're disappointed. You want to stay at the playground longer and we're starting home now." Did they put the blame on you for having expectations and desires? "Who do you think you are to want that toy! Of course we're not buying it for you." Did they teach you to swallow your feelings? "I'll give you something to cry about!"

When they experienced disappointment, did they treat themselves with care, or blame themselves, or lash out at someone else? How did they behave when they were disappointed in you? Was that rare, or constant?

Quiet attention. We naturally internalize the voices of the adults around us and continue to treat ourselves as they treated us, and as they treated themselves. We can interrupt this pattern by pausing, noticing the internalized voices, and choosing a different response. We can give quiet attention to our experience, accepting that this is how it is right now. We are allowed to be affected by not getting what we want.

If you were shamed or punished for disappointment, you might feel an urgent need to erase it or distract yourself. It might take time to separate the reflexive cascade of shame or fear or anger from the feeling of disappointment itself.

When you pause and breathe into disappointment, you might feel tightness in your throat, heaviness in your belly, ache in your heart, mouth turned down, or other responses in your body. Your mind might race to figure out a way to fix the problem or assign blame. You might feel deflated or weighed down. What do you notice?

Adjust expectations. When you take time to sit with a disappointment, acknowledgement might be enough, or you might feel the need to take further action to resolve it.

Disappointment is a mismatch between our expectations and outcomes. One way to resolve disappointment is to adjust our expectations. We can call ahead to the hardware store to check their stock. We can remind the friend ahead of time. We can keep applying to jobs until one comes through. We can work for voting rights for the next election.

We can choose, after a series of disappointments, to stop trying. Go to a different hardware store. Call a different friend. Apply for jobs in a different city. Put our efforts toward a different cause. No one can decide for us where that threshold is. We hold out hope for change until something shifts inside, and then we turn our attention elsewhere.

Keep healthy entitlement. Disappointment can lead us to question our right to expect anything at all. We wrestle with healthy entitlement when our expectations and environment are out of sync. It can help to seek nourishing feedback that supports a balanced sense of what we deserve and can expect.

Enough as we are. When we receive too much criticism and not enough delight, we internalize a sense that we are a disappointment. Perhaps we did not meet our family's expectations for education, career, relationship, or other external measures of success. Perhaps the effects of trauma interrupted pursuit of those goals. Perhaps we have different goals. Perhaps naming abusive dynamics puts us awkwardly at odds with the people whose approval we still secretly want. It can be hard to remember that our value does not depend on our achievements or abilities.

When we are healing from trauma, we might be disappointed that we still have limits and get triggered even after years of work. We might be disappointed when we go through another round of a recurring pattern. We might need to take a break from healing and ease our expectations of ourselves and our healing process.

Get some distance. It makes sense to veer away from the pain of feeling like we are a disappointment. Perhaps we can acknowledge tiny bits of that feeling. Perhaps we can sit with the small child inside who feels that way, providing a kind witness but not drowning in the feeling itself. Perhaps we can put the feeling a little distance away, over by the wall, still acknowledged in the room, but not right on top of us.

When we can get some space from that feeling, we can also find the truth that we are enough just as we are, not a disappointment at all.

Disappointment in someone else can be almost as painful, especially if it feels like their actions show disrespect or not valuing us. Often, people's actions are about themselves, not about us. It still hurts not to be seen, heard, and valued, even if someone is caught up in their own issues. We might find relief when we can let go of the expectation for change.

Catastrophic disappointments. Some disappointments are catastrophic, traumatic in themselves. We get served divorce papers, or laid off without warning, or evicted from our home, or deported from a mandatory courthouse appearance. Our whole life changes. We need to grieve the old life even as we struggle to establish a new one. We might have a spiritual crisis if we believe at some level that bad things only happen to people who deserve them.

Catastrophic disappointments rearrange our view of the world and our place in it. We digest them a little at a time, and reach out for all the help and support we can find.

Choose your story. The effect of a disappointment depends a lot on the story we tell about it. Choose a narrative with room for hope. Instead of, "I never get what I want," choose, "I didn't get what I wanted this time." Instead of, "There is something wrong with me," or "I deserved it," choose, "I have skills to learn and experience to gain."

Disappointment is part of life. We are led to believe that if we do everything right and have the right attitude, we will not be disappointed. At the same time, if we are rarely disappointed, perhaps we could expect more and take more risks. Disappointment can be a gateway to what we do want. When we can sit with disappointment, we find our balance between acceptance and efforts toward change.

Make Room for Grief

Grief is emotional pain in response to a loss. "Something is missing!" It can be knife-sharp and overwhelming, or a dull ongoing ache. Unlike sadness, which can be about something happening to someone else, grief is visceral, personal, immediate. It can include heartbreak, bitter disappointment, and rage at the unfairness of loss.

Wail aloud. Grief wants to wail aloud and writhe and rub dirt in our hair. It wants to be fully felt by the person grieving. It wants to be witnessed and acknowledged by the community. Grief can be private, but it is not meant to be secret.

In our modern society, we assign active, loud grief only to children. As adults, we curl around our grief, stifle it, stuff it down, make it small and silent and invisible. It leaks from between our concealing fingers as silent tears when no one is looking. Compacted grief leaches the joy out of being alive, and looks a lot like depression.

Affected by loss. Because we do not see others grieving, we feel hijacked by our powerful emotions. We criticize ourselves for not pulling it together, rather than turning toward ourselves with compassion for our pain. We gaslight ourselves, telling ourselves that the good parts of what we lost were not really there, or that it is our fault for reaching for what we wanted and daring to be happy. We believe we should not be affected by losing what we love.

When we lose an attachment figure, someone who supplied warmth and joy and above all a sense of safety and belonging, the loss feels like an essential part of us has been ripped away. We have to learn to live around the gaping hole left behind.

Unpredictable. The length and intensity of grief does not necessarily correspond to the apparent severity of the loss. A "small" loss can trigger an avalanche of stored grief as we try to stuff it into an internal closet that is already full. We might have pinned our hopes for the future or our steadiness in the present on what is now gone.

Like a harsh winter or a bad case of the flu, grief can last far longer than we want it to. We expect the sharpness of grief for a big loss to abate after a month. Instead, it might ease after the first year of painful anniversaries, and might continue long after that.

Grief has its own rhythm and timetable inside each of us. It might be shorter than we expect, or resolve suddenly into a half-forgotten lightness. It can be as hard to give ourselves permission to stop grieving as it is to step into grieving fully. We might believe that it is disloyal to feel better.

Progress is uneven, small reprieves followed by sudden resurgences. Reminders and associations slowly wear away over months, until one day we realize we got through that painful reminder while thinking of something else entirely.

Grief disrupts our plans and gets in the way of productivity and accomplishments. Grieving can be a full-time job. We have to adjust our expectations and make room for grief to move through us.

At the same time, grief is a normal part of being alive and connected. Random, unfair, cruel loss can happen to any of us, no matter how hard we work to make the "right" choices. Blaming the victim does not protect us from the pain of loss.

Other griefs. Not all grief is about loss of something we had. It might be grief for something we never had at all, like attuned parenting or warm community or a safe childhood. We can acknowledge the pain of what is missing and take in small bits of attunement or community or safety in our current lives.

Some of our grief might be for big losses that we are all experiencing together. Catastrophic pandemic. Whole species silenced forever. Thriving open spaces razed and covered with concrete. Increasing climate chaos as we pour more and more heat into the system. Increasing inequality and people around us suffering without access to housing, food, and medical care. We can join together to mourn our losses and resist where we can.

Loneliness. Just as we do not learn how to be with our own grief, we do not learn how to be with others who are grieving. At a time when we most need companionship and support, grief can be compounded by friends who back away when they do not know what to say, or who fear grief might be catching when they feel their buried grief stirring. Loneliness and grief often go together and intensify each other.

We can look for support groups or grief rituals where people know how to hear us and lean toward us rather than away.

Turn toward ourselves. We can turn toward our grieving self and be our own caring friend. No matter what we are grieving and how our internal and external Feelings Police think we "should" be handling it, we can take time to let our feelings move through us. We can offer ourselves physical care with water, food, sleep, and movement. We can take emotional care of ourselves by keeping our grief company and allowing it to be just as it is. We can write out our feelings in private journals and online forums.

We can also reach for distractions. There is a balance between honoring our emotions and taking breaks from them. Grief is something to live into, not grit our teeth through. We can continue with activities we used to enjoy, or start something new. Spending time outside can be helpful, even if it is a brief walk around the block. We can make order in our living space, which can be soothing when so much feels out of our control.

We can create rituals for ourselves, such as telling a rock how we feel and then placing it in running water. We can talk to a photo of a person we lost. We can choose to wear black for a year. We can choose to wear bright colors that cheer us up. Grief is as individual and as universal as a fingerprint.

Kindness and warmth. Moment by moment, we can accompany ourselves through acute and chronic grief with kindness and warmth. Eventually, it softens. Eventually, it becomes the background rather than the foreground. Not erased, but integrated into who we are as we continue to move through our lives.

3: Uncomfortable Emotions

Resonate with Loneliness

Emotional warmth is defined as being met or meeting others with affection and welcome, with a feeling of being cared for, nourished, and nurtured.

The book *Your Resonant Self* makes the extraordinary assertion that some people's default inner voice gives them ongoing emotional warmth.* For those of us who did not have emotionally warm parents in the past, nor an emotionally warm partner in the present, it would be wonderful to be able to access emotional warmth while alone.

Embodied understanding. Resonance is defined as sensing that another being fully understands us and sees us with emotional warmth and generosity. Resonance between two people is participatory, present, embodied, and active. It is easier to achieve resonance when we allow our emotions out to the edges of our bodies, where they can be sensed through our facial expressions and voice and body language.

The other person allows our emotions and experiences to move them (but not overwhelm them) like a sounding board physically vibrating with an incoming sound. They welcome us warmly, and we feel that in return.

Words can help reinforce the essential nonverbal signals of taking in, understanding, and accepting. "Yes, that makes sense. I hear you. You seem really angry." Those words could be warmly resonant, or coldly distancing. Our bodies feel the difference.

---
* *Your Resonant Self*, W. W. Norton & Co., 2017, by Sarah Peyton.

Resonant anger. I experienced resonance when I shared a recent encounter. "I stopped to move a yard waste bin out of the bike lane, and the homeowner came out to yell at me for leaning my bike against his tree. He said there was plenty of room left for bikes in the lane." The listener said, "That's ridiculous!" My body relaxed as I received her resonant anger. I felt her warm understanding and affirmation that I deserve to take up space in the bike lane, and I deserve to take up space telling the story.

Early affection. Babies need carers to resonate with their experiences, reflect them back affectionately, and help them find words for the experiences over time. When we miss out on early resonance, we are left with an uncertain void where there could be a solid core of self-support.

We internalize not only how our early carers treat us, but also how they treat themselves. Our nervous system senses theirs and absorbs, "This is how to be in the world." Perhaps they never learned warmth themselves. Perhaps they passed along a sense of not fitting in. Fortunately our brain and nervous system remain malleable and we can continue to learn new patterns as adults.

Grow your Inner Nurturer. *Your Resonant Self* invites us to connect with a Resonant Self Witness, a part of our brain that listens and responds warmly to our experience. In Inner Relationship Focusing, Ann Weiser Cornell calls this Self-in-Presence.* I call this part our Inner Nurturer.

You can grow your Inner Nurturer by gathering together memories of anyone who has been warm to you, or delighted in your presence, or resonated with your experience. Let

---

* "Inner Relationship Focusing" by Ann Weiser Cornell and Barbara McGavin.
https://focusingresources.com/inner-relationship-focusing/

your body remember how that felt. Also gather memories of feeling warm kindness toward someone, perhaps a friend or a small child or a pet. Let your body remember that feeling.

Let those feelings of warmth and kindness coalesce into a presence inside. Perhaps you want to visualize meeting this presence in a safe place, a secret room in your house or a bench in a beautiful garden or an island only you know about. Maybe the presence is a grandmother whose kind eyes see all the way into you and smile. Maybe the presence has square shoulders and strong arms that protect you. Maybe the presence is a soft cat or a tall tree or a gentle flame.

Practice warmth. Whenever you connect with that presence, you reinforce the parts of your brain and nervous system that generate warm kindness, and make that kindness more available to the parts of you that feel small and alone and broken.

Practice bringing warm understanding to all your experiences, including accomplishments, mistakes, frustration and self-criticism. Your Inner Nurturer might feel like spaciousness, room in your chest for all your emotions to bounce around and eventually find rest. It might feel like a teacher who treats her students with affection and respect even when she is angry with them. It might feel like a friend who says, "It's not you!"

Turn toward loneliness. If you cannot find resonance, turn toward that jarring experience itself. How does it feel inside? It might be a familiar feeling of loneliness and not being understood. Notice how that is for you with as much gentleness as you can. What do you feel in your body? What thoughts and emotions come along with it?

There is a lot of loneliness around trauma. Growing up with abusive or neglectful parents is fundamentally lonely.

Our nervous system spends more time in fight-or-flight and less time in social engagement. We struggle to learn how to connect with others when our system is busy managing high levels of distress. We cannot talk openly about what is happening at home, partly because we lack the words.

When trauma happens later, we struggle with taboos around talking about distress, and difficulties with settling our nervous system enough to be social.

Not a punishment. We have taboos around talking about loneliness, too. There are pervasive myths that loneliness goes away if we think about it the right way, or if we learn the right skills, or if we reach out enough to others, or if we become part of a couple. Yes, it helps to work toward enjoying our own company and to reach out to others when we can. At the same time, we are social mammals, and we will long for resonance when it is missing.

Loneliness is not a punishment, nor a judgment about being too broken for community. Loneliness simply is. We can bring kind resonance to our experience of loneliness. This is how the heartache feels right now. Here is the bitterness that goes with it. It makes sense that we feel that way. It makes sense that loneliness hurts.

When we feel lonely for a specific person, we can warmly ask our attention to stay with our experience of missing them, rather than focusing on them. When we notice our attention wandering away, we can kindly ask it to return. Every time we turn toward our experience with warmth, we strengthen our Inner Nurturer.

Turn toward fear. While it sounds wonderful to be met with resonance, it might bring up fear or anger. We might remember being unwillingly drawn toward warmth like a hungry stray dog toward food, only to experience entrapment and more abuse when we get close. We might feel shame for wanting closeness and for having needs at all. We might believe that wanting warmth makes us responsible for being abused, even though wanting warmth is part of being a mammal, and the abuser is always responsible for abusing. We can quietly, gently sense how that fear or anger feels inside and keep it company.

Accompaniment. Our Inner Nurturer can bring accompaniment, the sense that we are not alone with our experience. Warm acceptance from inside us can counteract shame and the feeling of being unacceptable, making it safer to experience all our uncomfortable emotions. When we can offer resonance to ourselves and others, we are making the world a better place one moment of connection at a time.

Resources

The Language of Emotions, Sounds True Publishing, 2010, by Karla McLaren contains detailed descriptions of emotions and how to work with them in a practical way.

Lost Connections, Bloomsbury Books, 2019, by Johann Hari is a journalist's personal and investigative account of depression.

Journey to the Dark Goddess, John Hunt Publishing, 2012, by Jane Meredith offers tools to work with catastrophic disappointments, which she compares to descents into the underworld.

Death Without Denial, Grief Without Apology, NewSage Press, 2016, by former Oregon Governor Barbara Roberts offers a loving clear-eyed unflinchingly personal look at terminal illness, death, and grief.

The Wild Edge of Sorrow, North Atlantic Books, 2015, by Francis Weller is a luminously poetic and thoughtful discussion of grief and how to acknowledge it with meditation and group rituals.

Tear Soup, Grief Watch Press, 2007, story by Pat Schwiebert and Chuck DeKlyen, illustrated by Taylor Bills. A compassionate book about grieving in children's book format, helpful for any age.

It's Ok That You're Not Ok, Sounds True, 2017, by Megan Devine is a compassionate and thorough exploration of catastrophic grief, including suggestions for helpers.

Your Resonant Self, W. W. Norton & Co., 2017, by Sarah Peyton has guided meditations on how to connect with yourself with warmth, based on neuroanatomy and Nonviolent Communication (NVC).

4: Full Self

Trauma interrupts and confuses our relationship with our bodies and ourselves. As we heal from trauma, we reclaim all of ourselves, all the way to our edges.

Growing up, we hear messages like, "Don't be too full of yourself," or "Who do you think you are?" Each person's job is to learn about ourselves and carve out space to thrive and grow.

Honor all the parts and voices inside you, including the ones who do not want to exist and the ones who fiercely guard your right to exist. Protect your boundaries and respect your limits. Know that you deserve to have your needs met with kindness, including your need for nourishment.

You are embodying hope by being yourself, and your full self pulls together to help you get through difficult times.

In Search of Self-Confidence

Self-confidence is not just about trusting our ability to accomplish tasks. When we lack self-confidence, we doubt that we deserve love, success, comfort, joy, happiness. At our core, we doubt that we deserve to exist.

Kind attention. When children receive kind, caring, responsive attention, it reinforces that they are intrinsically valuable and worthy of taking up space. When children's feelings are accurately reflected back to them, they learn to trust the validity of their inner experience. For example, "It looks like you're really mad right now." With congruence between their inner truths and outer responses, children develop a solid confidence at their core.

Missing reflections. In contrast, violent or contemptuous behavior toward children is jarringly incongruent with their intrinsic value. In too many homes, feelings are ignored, invalidated, or punished. An angry child is met with, "Wipe that frown off your face!" or "Calm down, everything is fine." Incongruent responses erode children's trust in their own experience, leaving uncertainty and shame at their core.

Gaslighting directly feeds that uncertainty. "This isn't happening," during abuse. Constantly shifting rules and punishments, without admitting that they are changing. Accusing the child of being crazy, broken, or wrong for being affected by abuse and neglect.

Emotional neglect can be subtle and corrosive. When adults are too dissociated or depressed to mirror a child's experience back to them, the child feels adrift, wondering what is real and how to get people to respond.

It is confusing and heartbreaking for children when they clearly signal their pain, but do not receive comfort and better care in response. They lose confidence that their well-being matters, and that sensing pain means care is needed.

External validation. When we lack inner certainty about our right to exist, we wistfully try to imitate other people's confident entitlement to take up space. We beat ourselves up for mistakes, real or imagined, as if they could possibly affect our intrinsic value.

We directly or indirectly ask others if we are okay. We agonize over silence or unkindness, and constantly seek out the next bit of reassurance. Contempt eats into us like acid because we are missing the neutralizing inner certainty that it is undeserved.

We recognize nourishment when a mentor, practitioner, friend, or lover reflects us warmly and positively, even if a part of us also pushes that away. Each bit of external approval or kind witnessing helps us build a stronger sense of self and eventually internalize our own Inner Nurturer.

Everyone grieves at the loss of a warm connection. The loss is more wrenching if the lost person takes our externally-based positive self-image with them. When we depend on someone else's positive view of us, it leads to enmeshment and difficulty leaving if the relationship becomes abusive. Some abusive relationships start with intentional "love-bombing" to hook in people with shaky self-confidence.

Sit with doubt. We feel shame for being so vulnerable around external validation, even though we all have a need for kind reflection. We cannot make our missing confidence appear simply by deciding we "should" have it. We can sit with our doubts and shame, take in available nourishment and support, and let inner confidence grow slowly over time.

Accurate reflections. We can gently connect with a part that doubts we deserve to exist. We can be our own kind witness and spend time with whatever we sense about that part. We can also make space for the inner voice that criticizes the doubting, hurting part, and any other voices that have reactions to that voice.

All parts of us are doing their best to help us survive. Many of them formed when we were young and had only a small repertoire of tools. When we learn about our emotions and provide our own accurate reflections, we begin to mend the holes left by inadequate parenting. "A part of me is mad right now."

Not about us. When people treat us with contempt, cruelty, or indifference, they are saying more about their internal state than about ours. Similarly, when we feel self-contempt, we have to be mindful not to project it unfairly on the people around us. No one intrinsically deserves contempt. While some damaging behaviors are contemptible, we want to minimize our use of contempt.

Self-confidence lets us keep our balance when others treat us badly. When we can stay even-tempered and kind, they have an opportunity to correct their behavior. We can also calmly communicate our boundaries. "We don't do that here." "I don't like that. Please stop." "Wow."

Unfortunately, some people do not take the hint. It is not our job to be endlessly nice in the face of bad behavior. Self-confidence sparks anger and self-protective action when someone continues to mistreat us.

Make the leap. When we can turn toward ourselves with care in the midst of feeling doubt and self-contempt, we make space for healing to occur. We naturally need care from others to show us the way, and we also need to make the leap to assert, "I do deserve to exist." Or at least, "I am going to treat myself as if I deserve to exist."

Cherish Your Limits

We affirm our right to exist when we honor our limits, which are part of being an embodied human mammal. We need rest, food, drink, and comfort at regular intervals to stay in balance. We can ignore those needs for a while, but there is a mounting cost to our well-being the longer we set them aside. Paying attention to our limits, like our sensitivities, helps us compassionately care for ourselves.

Out of spoons. With youth and the privilege of an able body, our limits might be far outside of what we want to do in a day, and we do not often encounter them at all. A strong, able person might intentionally push their limits with a wilderness adventure, a marathon, or other challenges.

With physical or emotional impairments, we encounter our limits in a more daily way. We might have the energy for either a shower or a neighborhood walk, but not both, and have to choose between them. We might have variable energy from day to day, making it difficult to plan ahead to get together with friends.

Spoon Theory* explains these limits by saying that people with chronic illness have a limited number of spoons per day, and each activity costs one or more spoons. A person who is out of spoons needs to rest and recover.

Limits are normal. We might feel frustrated when limits

---

* Christine Miserandino developed Spoon Theory to explain to a friend what it is like to have lupus. https://butyoudontlooksick.com/articles/written-by-christine/the-spoon-theory/

get in the way of what we want to accomplish. Encouraged by consumer culture's quest for more better faster yesterday, we might feel shame at having more limits than "normal," even though having limits is perfectly normal for each of us.

We can unlearn the ableism of thinking that people with impairments are less worthy in any way. We can choose to avoid ableist metaphors such as "crazy" for evil behavior, "lame" for lack of effort, and "blind" for unobservant. Our limits are not bad, and do not make us bad people.

We each create our lives within the constraints that our limits provide. A container garden on a balcony is as vital as a garden spanning acres. Much of the harm of our limits comes from the disgraceful lack of social services and support for people with physical, emotional, or financial limits.

Trauma adds limits. Trauma can introduce limits suddenly, for example through physical injury from a car crash or emotional injury from betrayal and assault. It takes time and energy to heal, leaving fewer resources for other activities. Survivors are faced with adapting to unfamiliar limits in addition to other changes wrought by trauma.

PTSD can shrink our world as we try to rest and avoid triggers. We receive messages to "Step outside your comfort zone!" and "Do something that scares you every day." Those messages apply to people who have a comfort zone to stay in. Instead, trauma survivors often need to slow down and find a sense of safety, rather than staying in a state of emergency.

Gentle experiments. It takes experimentation to discover our soft and hard limits. When we start feeling tired, maybe we can push on and rest more later, or maybe we need to stop right then to avoid days of increased pain or panic. It is an inherent part of the process to get it wrong sometimes in both directions, either becoming exhausted, or skipping an activity that might have been possible after all.

When we carefully test our limits, we might find that we can comfortably go farther than we thought. When we raise an arm slowly, we might be able to reach overhead with a previously injured shoulder. When we have the option to leave at any time, we might have a good time at a party that would previously have been intolerably crowded and loud.

Allow mistakes. With variable limits that increase as we heal, or decrease with a progressive condition, there is even more experimentation and possible mistakes. It helps to be gentle with ourselves as we try to predict what we can do each day. Over time, we learn to recognize our subtle signs of "enough."

Most of all, we need to be attentive to our limits around taking risks, even small ones. When we over-stretch, the body lets us know with an emotional meltdown, sudden illness, or back spasm. Each body has its vulnerabilities and its ways of communicating, "Too much!"

Refill the well. As hard as it is to say "No" or "Maybe later" or "I need a break" or "I need help" when we are working on our own goals, it can be even harder when we are disappointing someone else, or doing less for a cause we care about. Women and other marginalized groups are socialized to subordinate our needs to the people around us.

Our core commitments need to include our own well-being along with commitments toward others and to making the world a better place. We are all entitled to honor our limits and refill our own well, especially in difficult times.

The Perils of Nice

Never take the last cookie. Avoid drama. Never tell people they are wrong. Wait for people to notice what you need. Smile at strangers.

We have a lot of rules about how to be nice, how to be liked, and how to navigate our limits with others. The details vary in each community, which can be surprising after moving to a new town. Generally, people seen as women face higher pressure to be nice and higher penalties for failing to be nice.

Smooth the way. Nice can be kind, respectful, courteous, helpful, patient, and considerate. On the negative side, nice can include waiting endlessly for our turn to speak and allowing ourselves to be interrupted without protest. It can include watching others take credit for our successful ideas and shift blame onto us for their mistakes. Nice means doing the emotional labor to smooth the way for everyone else.

Nice means not making other people feel bad, even though we cannot control what someone else feels. Nice means not being too smart or capable, in case that makes someone else feel small. Nice means not stretching to our full capacity, physically or metaphorically. Nice means not taking up too much space.

No boundaries. Nice people do not express boundaries, preferences, or needs. Asking for accommodation for sensitivities or other disabilities might cause inconvenience. Even when we express boundaries, nice people definitely do not enforce them. People deserve more chances! After all, we are not perfect ourselves.

Nice people think positive thoughts about others, even in the face of mounting negative effects. In particular, nice people do not report abuse. Nice people do not even think of it as abuse, but rather wonder what they might have done to cause someone to treat them that way.

Accept what you get. Nice means being satisfied with what you have, even if you are not being heard. Nice means that if you feel disappointed, you tell yourself your expectations were out of line.

Nice means using up every bit of your energy and strength and time trying to make that job or relationship or living situation work, and then being blamed for being exhausted and stressed. Nice means not being affected by past trauma, never letting on that you need treatment and care.

No anger. Above all, nice people do not get angry, frustrated, irritable, grumpy, or in any way unpleasant to be around. Nice people do not take up other people's time with their gripes, nor get annoyed when they are treated badly.

Nice smiles uncomfortably at that racist or sexist joke rather than saying, "Wow," or "Hey, that's not funny," because speaking up would cause drama. It is not nice to confront bigotry.

Welcomed and included. Nice does have its rewards. Nice people are welcomed and included just about everywhere. Nice people fit in, and get to feel good enough and "normal." We grieve for the consequences of not being nice enough, for our inability to fold ourselves small enough to fit into that box.

Masks badness. Abuse survivors often struggle with feeling like a terrible person, or like something is terribly wrong inside. Being nice can feel like an essential mask for that (illusory) inner badness. The Inner Critic or a whole internal committee can enforce niceness by cruelly criticizing any non-nice behavior.

When we struggle with a sense of not deserving anything, it is hard to endure pushback for asserting needs or boundaries. Any conflict can feel dangerous, even when it is a normal part of negotiating competing needs.

Speak truth kindly. Rather than following strict rules to be nice, we can find ways to speak our truth kindly. Kindness can set boundaries, assert preferences, and ask for what we need while remaining aware of the impact on others. It takes ongoing work to discern kind actions in complicated, conflicted situations. If we feel a healthy entitlement to get our needs met, it is easier to navigate environments where we receive criticism for not being nice enough.

Embrace difficult qualities. When we choose to speak out, it can be painful to hear that we are rude, harsh, selfish, critical, mean, difficult, judgmental, or scary. Since we all contain all qualities, we can work with owning the qualities that sting the most. "Yes, I can be harsh." Remember that you contain the opposite, too. "I can also be gentle." Look for examples of both, in yourself and others.

Hold yourself and your qualities with compassion. Those accusatory words carry gifts. Rude can be direct. Judgmental can be discerning. Selfish can be self-protective.

Open the trap. When our needs are not being met, the requirement to be nice can create a trap where we feel that either we have to accept the situation exactly as it is, or we have to leave the situation behind completely. When we are willing to be seen as harsh or difficult, we have more room to discern our needs and take steps toward meeting them, including asking others for changes. This opens space for the situation to improve gradually or end more gently.

Unfortunately, women in leadership positions experience the double bind of being judged as too abrasive and confrontational for their leadership qualities of strength, directness, decisiveness, and competence, or they are judged as too nice and thus not leadership material.

Power of authenticity. Being nice has the benefit of social approval and the perils of doing a lot of emotional labor and still not getting our needs met. When we do not constrain ourselves to be nice, we can step into the power of showing up as our authentic selves. Over time, we learn to wield that power kindly and creatively.

Balance for Your Inner Guardian

When faced with abusive parents or authoritarian medical practitioners, we learn that we have to be nice enough and submissive enough to receive care.

I do not run my bodywork practice that way. When I check in with a new client about how their body feels about being on the table, they often report that they feel tense, guarded, wary. Their body is still gathering information about whether this new environment is safe, and they are not yet ready to trust my good intentions.

It might be the first time they have had permission to check in with their body and take all the time they need to give unforced consent to be touched. They feel relieved when I give them plenty of space to get to know this Inner Guardian who protects their boundaries. Some clients report an ongoing struggle between a fierce Inner Guardian and the parts of them that are in pain and want help.

Internalized protection. Ideally, an Inner Guardian is an internalized version of lovingly protective adults around a growing child. When adults intervene to protect a child when needed, and also step back to let the child take action on their own, the child learns to both ask for help and rely on their own strength. Their Inner Guardian continues learning skills and flexibility from the examples around them.

Desperate measures. When a child does not have protection and is repeatedly exposed to bullying or abuse, a part of them learns to stand guard out of desperation. This part presents a strong front to the outside world and shelters the terrified child parts inside.

This Inner Guardian tends to be frozen in time, a young child acting older than their years. The Guardian might present as more masculine than the child as a whole if the child believes that masculinity is required for fierceness and strength.

If school is safer than home, the Inner Guardian might march the child to school on time and make sure homework gets done. Some Inner Guardians rely on intellectual strength rather than physical strength to figure out the rules and stay safe.

All or nothing. Young children are prone to all or nothing thinking. An overwhelmed Inner Guardian might divide the world into abusers and good people, holding themselves responsible for figuring out which is which. Sadly, warning signs are easy to discern in hindsight, but are less clear in advance. Abusers do often start with small boundary violations to test a victim. At the same time, there is a high social cost to responding forcefully to every small boundary violation.

In truth, most of us are in the messy middle, trying our best to be good people and sometimes causing harm. Even people who are intentional predators will have friends and communities who vouch for them.

Rather than trying to classify people as good or bad, we can classify behavior as working for us or not. If someone's behavior does not work for us, we can try to find ways to tolerate it, ask for change, or distance ourselves from the situation, without assigning labels.

Separate past and present. If we witness someone behaving in a predatory way, the first step is to protect ourselves in the present. Then we can notice differences between present and past. It is easy to get triggered into feeling panicked and helpless when someone's behavior reminds us of past abuse. With our adult resources, we have the options of comforting our scared inner parts, naming the predatory behavior to others, and offering support to people targeted by predation.

Some Inner Guardians carry the belief from childhood that there is no help available and they have to take care of every problem by themselves. Other parts' needs for rest and care might be embarrassing and disallowed. An Inner Guardian might also be exhausted and long for enough safety to be able to rest.

Guarding others. Inner Guardians are often reserved around other people. They can also be warmly protective when someone seems vulnerable. This can lead to polarized relationships where one person's Inner Guardian is relating to another person's fragile inner child. The relationship can fracture abruptly when someone expresses qualities outside their assigned role, vulnerability on the Guardian side or strength on the child side. This can trigger intense feelings of betrayal and abandonment.

Sense your Inner Guardian. We can relate to others in a more balanced way when our vulnerable inner children are protected by our own Inner Guardian. Are you already familiar with the part of you that asserts boundaries and calls out injustice? Maybe your Inner Guardian helps you follow the rules and keep your head down. Your Inner Guardian might stand strong in your legs and curl your fists, or shield your back, or live in your head, figuring things out.

Especially for women, an Inner Guardian's actions can bring disapproval for not being sufficiently compliant, cooperative, or submissive. An Inner Guardian can get buried in the effort to be nice, fit in, and get along. What do you notice inside if you give yourself permission to be strong, fierce, or angry?

Covert action. Buried Inner Guardians can act covertly, pushing away opportunities that feel too risky and people who get too close. Do you notice a part of you that wants to protect you, but is acting out of step with your conscious goals?

Inner Guardians can constrict inside, causing chronic tightness and pain in their efforts to protect us or hold us back. They can flare in response to perceived invasion, which leads to sensitivities and a narrowed window of tolerance for change, discomfort, or unfamiliar situations.

Listen warmly. Take some time to listen to your Inner Guardian. You might sense a strong presence that speaks up right away, or a vague sense in the background that takes a while to become clearer. Offer resonant warmth and acceptance to what you hear. Perhaps it will let you know what it wants and does not want for you, from its point of view.

You do not need to argue, bargain, placate, or convince the Inner Guardian of anything. If voices leap in with opinions, listen kindly to them as well.

You might hear about panicked struggles for control in an effort to create reliable safety. You might hear about the terror of repeated betrayals that makes it impossible to let go and trust people in authority.

You might hear a child's despair at being outmatched and helpless when boundaries were violated. This can lead to either shutting down or using full force when feeling threatened.

You might hear about old rules like, "If I don't stand up for myself well enough, it's my fault if I get abused." Let the

Inner Guardian know that you hear the old rule, and the pain it has caused. Stay aware that while standing up for oneself might cause some abusers to reconsider, the abuser is responsible for the choice to commit abuse.

Balance in the present. As you build a connection with your Inner Guardian by listening warmly, it can begin to notice your current body size, skills, and resources. As it becomes more integrated into the present, you can bring more balanced, skillful responses to present-time threats.

Healthy Entitlement: Discern Your Domain

Children instinctively know they deserve care and protection. Each infant is born with a full-body knowing that they are entitled to nourishment, shelter, rest, and loving contact. Each baby vigorously pursues their wants with all the resources at their disposal, crying, reaching out when they want something, and turning away when they have had enough. Their carer's task is to provide for those needs.

Unless they have been abused or neglected, small children are still in solid contact with their inner feelings and wants, and pursue them with their greatly expanded repertoire of words and actions. Their carer's task is to provide for their needs, and also begin to teach them a reciprocal respect for others' needs.

Both external and internal. As we grow older, we acquire a sense of our domain, the part of the world we are entitled to make choices about. We learn what we can expect to receive and what we can take for granted. Entitlement is partly a social process guided by external feedback, and partly an internal process guided by our sense of what we need and deserve.

Our bodies belong to us. We are entitled to complete autonomy over the insides and surfaces of our bodies. What happens inside an adult's body is solely that person's business. Children's bodily autonomy should be respected as much as possible from the beginning.

- **Food.** As Ellyn Satter firmly states, at every age we get to choose what and how much food we eat.* For children, adults control what foods are offered and when. As adults, we both procure food for ourselves, and check inside about what and how much we want to eat at each meal or snack. Different kinds and amounts of food work for different people. A large range of body sizes, from skinny to fat, are normal for those who have them. Food is a personal choice.
- **Sensations.** We each have a unique set of sensitivities and sensations as we interact with the world. Some people's eyes see much farther into the infrared spectrum than average. Some people have migraines, intense pain that is not measurable from the outside. Some people are irritated by clothing materials, noise levels, or light levels that are comfortable for others. We get to trust our senses.
- **Emotions.** Our many shades of anger, sadness, joy, and fear are physiological messages about our environment, both past and present. We get to feel how we feel.
- **Desires.** Our desires and aversions are internal pointers to what works well for us. Our dreams are ours to nurture. We get to want what we want.
- **Safety.** Our body belongs to us. No one should harm us. No one should touch us in any way without our explicit consent.

Even these basic entitlements to bodily autonomy are subject to challenge and debate for people with less privilege. We police people's food choices and feelings. We cast doubt

---

* *Secrets of Feeding a Healthy Family*, Kelcy Press, 1999, by Ellyn Satter.

on people's senses. We blame victims and support rape culture instead of holding rapists accountable and teaching everyone to respect consent.

Entitlement depends on circumstances. Entitlement to domains outside our bodies varies widely. Some people struggle to guard a few possessions while experiencing homelessness. Some people control large estates. Some people have jobs with very little control over conditions and hours. Some people control vast businesses where they dictate the lives of many others.

Everyone's views of entitlement are distorted by the funhouse mirror of feedback received from others. A child of narcissistic parents is punished for having any wants or needs at all, and learns to shrink back at the first hint of judgment. An internal voice says, "Not allowed to want that! Needs are bad! You're too much!"

People with more privilege are socialized to expect more space, more credibility, more tolerance, more favors, more authority, and more success than average. From this privileged stance, someone with less privilege claiming basic bodily autonomy and respect looks like "too much entitlement." We all need to adjust our expectations so that everyone's bodies are entitled to respect and care.

Flexible, changing balance. Healthy entitlement firmly claims bodily autonomy. When our wants and needs affect other people, we monitor those effects and negotiate a flexible, changing balance with other people's healthy entitlement. We expect to get what we want some of the time, but not all the time. We expect our wants and needs to be treated with respect, even when they are not met.

For example, we all share a need to get from one place to another safely, and we want to get there on time. Too much entitlement says, "I'm in a hurry, so I drive at reckless speeds, and run lights that are turning red. Cyclists and pedestrians should just keep out of my way." Healthy entitlement says, "Everyone has an equal right to the road, so I drive courteously, stay aware of all road users, and move forward assertively when it is my turn."

Widen the scope. When people's needs are in conflict, it can help to widen the scope of the problem. How would it be possible for everyone to get what they need? Where can additional resources and support be brought in? In the case of transportation, planning for an extra five minutes of travel time relieves pressure and allows for more courteous driving.

Sometimes, needs are in conflict and there is no clear path toward resolution. We can invite a wider narrative and wait for a new insight or some other change to open a new path in the situation.

Our needs are not always the most important, nor the least important. It would be comforting to have a fixed answer to, "What am I entitled to?" We want to avoid the shame of overstepping our bounds, and yet we become trapped in constricted misery when we deny our entitlement to our experience and body.

Ongoing questioning. Healthy entitlement includes both body-centered certainty, and ongoing questioning as we interact with others. We might feel outraged when someone denies an entitlement we took for granted. We might feel deep relief when someone supports an entitlement we did not know we had.

For example, someone who is used to speaking at length in meetings might be startled and offended by being asked to step back. Someone who is used to being silenced might feel a sense of physical expansion when invited to speak.

Healthy entitlement is catching. When we associate with people who treat themselves and others with consistent respect, we learn to claim our domain respectfully. Since most of us are immersed in racist, patriarchal, oppressive cultures, we also have to consciously study anti-racism, feminism, intersectionality, and other forms of equity to thoughtfully question our unexamined privileges.*

---

* See "Resources" on page 70 for a starting reading list.

Your Body is Your Ally

Even though we are entitled to care and protection, it is painfully easy to blame our bodies for trauma we endure. Perhaps if we had looked or acted differently, the trauma would not have happened. Afterwards, we want the body to just get over it instead of needing a long healing process. We disconnect from our bodies, and then feel surprised and betrayed by their insistent needs.

A large part of healing from trauma is making contact with your body, living in your body, being your body. This body, right now, with its actual size and shape and quirky mix of abilities and disabilities. This body, with its sensations and preferences and needs and desires.

Learned body judgment. Many of us get explicit messages as we grow up that there is something wrong with our bodies. Even if adults expressed delight in our child bodies exactly as they were right then and as they continued to change, society quickly steps in to tell us we are too much of this and not enough of that and (especially for girls and women) our worth is based on being pleasing to look at (by men). We absorb body judgment and body hatred and continue to wield them against ourselves.

If there was abuse or neglect or pain, the body soon feels like an enemy to flee rather than an ally to rest in. When the nervous system screams "danger! danger!" and no one helps soothe it, we learn to dissociate rather than to live in harmony with our physical self.

Buried needs. Some people are lucky enough to grow up in environments where needs and wants were matter-of-factly accepted and mostly met. We all deserve to grow up in an environment where hunger is met with food, distress is met with soothing, and longing for touch is met with cuddles and hugs.

Most of us learned that at least some of our wants and needs were not okay, either through direct punishment or indirect withdrawal. Children learn to prune away or deeply bury the parts of them that do not make their carers happy, even if those parts are essential. Instead of mourning our unmet needs, we judge our bodies as bad for having them.

When we focus on our bodies as an enemy to be subdued rather than an ally to be tended, we skew our whole life experience toward battle and discomfort. In particular, trying to make ourselves physically smaller distracts us from taking up space as our full selves.

Myth of individualism. Mainstream US culture encourages us to look inward to solve problems. There is a myth that we can each individually control our lives and our bodies to resolve any issues that arise. In fact, our lives are tangled skeins of influences from past and present, a mix of the people, culture, environment, and oppressions surrounding us.

We can identify which parts of our lives are under our control by experimenting and noticing when our actions create change.

We can influence our bodies, but they are very much not under our control. Weight-loss diets do not work long-term for the vast majority of people, although they might work in the short term, giving us an illusion of control and effectiveness.*

Body size is complex. Our body size is the outcome of a complex set of factors, including our genetics, our feelings of safety or threat, our gut health, our available movement choices, and our available food choices. Most of those factors are not under our control. We can caringly do our best to choose movement and food that nourish us in each moment, and let our size and weight take care of themselves.

Even when we make grudging peace with the body we have, we might continue to wish we were smaller or stronger or taller or otherwise more socially acceptable. We are judged for how we look all the time. An internal critical voice repeats those judgments in an effort to keep us safer. It takes time to notice that voice rather than merging with it, and even more time for it to quiet down.

Fantasy of being different. In The Fantasy of Being Thin described by Kate Harding, we imagine that once we are thin, we will be a different, more capable person.† Instead, we can work to accept ourselves as we are now, and take action toward the life we want from that starting point. Similarly, we might have a Fantasy of Being Healed. While a lot gets better in healing from trauma, we do not turn into a different person with a different past.

If our body size does change, we might be physically reminded of other times in our lives when we were smaller or larger. Being smaller can feel childlike, vulnerable and exposed.

Notice what works. You can turn toward your body in a

---

* "Why Diets Don't Work" by Michelle Allison, November 19, 2013. https://fatnutritionist.com/index.php/why-diets-dont-work/

† *Lessons From the Fat-o-sphere*, Penguin Putnam Trade, 2009, by Kate Harding and Marianne Kirby.

friendly way by noticing what works or feels good right now. At the very least, you are breathing. Let your attention rest on the in and out of your breath, and notice what comes up.

When you first reconnect, you might encounter how it feels to be disconnected, or the distress that caused you to disconnect originally. Let that move through, and keep returning to the in and out of breath. Hold the thought that your body is already doing its best and it is okay just the way it is.

Your body deserves care. It might take repeated efforts to connect in a friendly way if you have been disconnected for a long time. Practice thinking of your body as a shy creature that deserves care and affection. Practice listening for and acknowledging sensations and needs.

When you connect, you might feel relief, and warmth, and an answering friendliness. Bodies are generally forgiving and want to feel connected.

Nourish and nurture. Listen for what feels nourishing and nurturing around food, movement, and rest. Notice what already feels good, and what you might want to do in addition. Make a list, and sit with it for a while.

When you are ready, experiment with giving yourself something from the list, and pay attention to how it feels. Sense for what feels good in the moment, and notice how you feel afterward. Some actions might have delayed effects, like delicious chocolate that keeps you from falling asleep later.

Feeling good physically or emotionally might be tied to shame or fear reactions. If brief good feelings were followed by more catastrophes in the past, you might need to build up your tolerance. Make small changes at first and ride out the reactions that are stirred up. Eventually, present safety will overwrite past associations.

Receive kindness. Your body holds your history, and your body also points faithfully toward what you need to heal. One of the big goals of healing is to feel better, and another is to be treated with kindness. Your body is you. When you tend to your body with generous care, you practice feeling better and receiving kindness right now.

Embody Hunger, Embody Fullness

As part of connecting more directly with our bodies just as they are right now, we can bring more awareness to eating, hunger, and fullness.

Soothing or stressful eating. Babies eat for comfort as well as nourishment. So do growing children and adults. Eating is a fundamental sensory pleasure and a direct way to soothe our nervous systems. Of all the ways to manage stress and overwhelming emotions, food is not a bad choice. We can add more tools for emotion management over time, and food will always remain a viable choice.

For many people, eating becomes associated with stress or pain rather than pleasure and comfort. Maybe mealtimes were filled with verbal abuse, or our jaw aches from past violence, or there was so much judgment and shaming that it is hard to know what to eat. In response, we dissociate from the whole process of eating.

Food keeps you alive. The most important purpose of eating is to sustain life. Since you are reading this, you are eating successfully. Bodies can be healthy in a wide range of sizes and shapes.* If you choose to bring more awareness to your eating, start with the knowledge that it is already good enough. You have good reasons to be doing exactly what you do.

---

* "Weight Science: Evaluating the Evidence for a Paradigm Shift," by Linda Bacon and Lucy Aphramor, January 24, 2011. https://nutritionj.biomedcentral.com/articles/10.1186/1475-2891-10-9

If those statements trigger an internal chorus of "Yes, buts!" about your health and size and attractiveness, simply listen. Notice how much inner yelling there is about your eating, how many rules and "shoulds." Let those voices know that you hear them and understand they are very concerned about your well-being. If a part of you flinches at being yelled at or argues back, let that part know that you hear it, too. Where in your body do you feel the yelling and responses?

Explore hunger. For most babies, barring neglect or physical issues, eating starts out simple. You got hungry and you ate. As a toddler, if you had choices, you noticed what you were hungry for and ate that. When you were full, you stopped.

Nowadays, hunger might feel dangerous, so you avoid feeling it. Or it might feel seductive, so you seek to prolong it. As an athlete, you might need to refuel your body before it signals hunger. If you have hypoglycemia or diabetes, you might need to keep careful track of how much food your body needs to keep functioning.

Notice the emotions and associations you have with hunger. Is it good, bad, neutral? What stories do you tell yourself about it? Pay attention to hunger and your responses to it as a kind observer.

Internal and external signals. How does hunger feel in your body? Is it an ache in your gut, or light-headedness, or belly rumbles? Is it increasing irritability and urgency? Is it depression and fogginess and sleepiness? Notice the physical sensations that alert you to the need to eat. If you have not noticed hunger in a long time, look for it with gentle curiosity.

What external signals trigger hunger inside you? Do you reliably get hungry at certain times of day? Do you get hungry when something smells good, or looks appealing? Does hunger arise when you are facing a task you do not quite know how to start, or an emotion you do not know how to manage? All these are fine reasons to be hungry.

Do you allow all of your hunger, or do you constrain it? Perhaps hunger is only allowed at certain times, or for certain amounts, and hunger for sweetness or comfort is frowned on. Do you tell your hunger it should be satisfied with less?

Explore fullness. Hunger is a biological signal to find and consume food. Its purpose is to be satisfied by comfortable fullness. If you are not in contact with the fullness signals inside, you might stop too soon and remain a little hungry, or stop too late and feel uncomfortably full.

What do you associate with fullness, with plenty, with freely eating as much as you want? Does it feel like your birthright? Or does it feel greedy, like you might not deserve it or you might be taking food away from others? If you worry about affording enough food for yourself and your household, imagine what it would be like to be relieved of that worry and have plenty for everyone. This is what we all deserve.

Fully welcome at any size. Contrary to everything we hear, eating does not directly determine body size, and your body size is normal for you. If you worry about gaining weight, imagine what it would be like to be relieved of that worry and be fully welcomed at any size. Imagine that you can find and afford clothes you like that fit you well. There is plenty of room for you everywhere, and you are treated with respect and care. This is what we all deserve.

Notice the emotions and associations you have with fullness. Is it good, bad, neutral? What stories do you tell yourself about it? Pay attention to fullness and your responses to it as a kind observer.

How does fullness feel in your body? What are your signals to stop eating? Do you guess what you might want and then finish the food on your plate? Do you pause to consider whether you want seconds? Do you eat more because it tastes good, or to keep someone company, or because it will be a while before you can eat again? All these are fine reasons to eat.

If you often eat to discomfort, or you feel compelled to keep eating even when you want to stop, or if you eat less than your body wants, you could gently explore your signals of fullness and your reasons for disconnecting from them.

When we notice that we engage in behaviors we cannot control, or we treat our bodies as enemies that must be controlled, we can kindly look for a part of us that is trying to protect us and survive using the few tools we had available when we were small. That part might be willing to learn new tools and even rest for a while when the present is safer than the past.

Experiments. As you explore hunger and fullness, you might choose to experiment with changing your usual patterns. Observe with kindness. Any result, including not wanting to do any experiments, is valuable information about your body and your self. Notice any hidden agendas you might have behind your experiments, like trying to change your size.

You might already pay close attention to everything you put in your mouth because of food sensitivities or other health issues. You might be numb around eating and not sense it at all. The pandemic may have introduced changes you would not otherwise have chosen. This is a chance to kindly observe the larger patterns of how you relate to food.

You could:
- Smell and look at your food before starting to eat, or dive right in.
- Bring your awareness to the inside of your mouth, or intentionally pay attention to other sensations as you eat.
- Chew a bite many more times or many fewer times than you usually do.
- Eat more slowly or more quickly than usual.
- Pause during a meal and check in with what you are feeling emotionally and physically.
- Eat with more people or fewer people than usual.

Closer to embodiment. When you allow yourself to embody your individual experience of hunger and fullness rather than pushing yourself to have the "right" experience, you move toward a kinder relationship with your body and your full self.

Resources

Go Only as Fast as Your Slowest Part Feels Safe to Go, Compassionate Ink, 2013, by Robyn Posin shares her discoveries about being with one's full self.

Taming Your Gremlin, HarperCollins Publishers, 2003, by Rick Carson talks about ways to get closer to the natural you, including not getting too caught up in your "pleasant person act."

Braving the Wilderness, Penguin Random House, 2019, by Brené Brown offers tips to balance strength and vulnerability as we find our path.

The Radical Acceptance of Everything, Calluna Press, 2005, by Ann Weiser Cornell and Barbara McGavin offers compassionate tools to work with inner parts.

Secrets of Feeding a Healthy Family, Kelcy Press, 1999, by Ellyn Satter is full of wise advice for adults trying to improve their eating competence.

Lessons From the Fat-o-sphere, Penguin Putnam Trade, 2009, by Kate Harding and Marianne Kirby is a kind, warm compendium of the authors' research-backed wisdom about giving up diets and actively cultivating a positive body image and self-acceptance.

Embodying Hope

5: Intricate Body

The elements of a body fit together like a house full of small soft rooms, all interconnected, one nestled against the next.

Our insides are mysterious to us. We can choose to explore the details of how our physical systems develop, function, and heal. We can learn to feel a surprising amount from the outside, using soft hands and friendly, attentive contact, and we can sense ourselves from the inside.

Bring curiosity to your explorations. Let yourself be a beginner at these new ways of sensing your body. You may not feel anything at first, or you may feel vague signals that you want to dismiss. Allow yourself to believe what you feel.

The more you connect with your nervous system, guts, lungs, sound production, and vision, the more you can appreciate and inhabit your intricate body.

The Push/Pull of Touch

Touch from others can be difficult for survivors of abuse, and has become more fraught with the Covid-19 pandemic. Many people have been deprived of touch as we avoid close contact with people outside our households. We can fill part of that gap with kind, non-sexual touch from our own hands.

Infants expect and require abundant joyful, loving touch. They continue to need the physical presence, warmth, heartbeat, and nervous system activity that surrounded them in the womb. When that drive to be held, rocked, soothed and comforted is met with enough touch and care, the child develops secure attachment.

Insecure attachment. If adults respond intermittently, the child develops anxious attachment, dedicating their whole being to figuring out how to entice adults into responding more consistently. If adults do not respond at all, the child develops avoidant attachment, shutting away their needs in the whole-body belief that touch will never come.

If adults both care for and harm the child, the child develop disorganized attachment, with equally compelling drives toward comforting touch and away from danger.

Natural need for touch. Adults also need touch. When the need for touch has been met well enough, with kindness and safety, we accept the ongoing need as naturally as we accept the need to breathe. It is simply part of us.

When we experienced absence or abuse from carers instead, we grow around an aching emptiness at our core.

5: Intricate Body

We cover it over with shame that somehow we were not enough to elicit caring touch. As we learn to explain the world to ourselves in words, an Inner Critic gives voice to that shame.

Damaged self-trust. When the need for touch pulls us toward people who also hurt us, our self-trust takes a beating. We feel unwillingly compelled and hijacked, ashamed of the inability to erase or ignore our touch hunger even though the need for touch is as physical as the need for air.

We also feel hijacked and ashamed when we flinch away from touch that appears harmless. We criticize ourselves for being affected by past harm. Touch can bring us into body awareness in the present moment, and it can also bring up vivid sensations from the past.

When a trusted adult sexually abuses a child, caring touch and sexual contact become deeply entangled. It can be difficult to disentangle them, especially since modern US culture provides few opportunities for non-sexual touch. It can help to seek out non-sexual caring touch from trusted friends, or bodywork, or activities like social dance or contact improv.

We wrestle for control over our need for touch and our responses to it. We search for safe, caring touch that can reach and calm the ongoing panicked distress of our inner infant. We try to listen to our conflicting inner signals for guidance.

Offer yourself touch. Even though the longing and confusion and fear is about touch from others, we can work on healing by turning toward ourselves. We can experiment with offering our own body caring non-sexual touch, and listen to all the reactions that arise.

Stay aware of consent from inside, and do not override a "no" or "don't want." Listening to "no" might be exactly what your body needs. You can also pay attention to the touch of your clothes, or the touch of water in the shower, or hug a tree, or cuddle a pet.

- Sense inside for what part of your body would like touch. Are there any parts that definitely do not want touch?
- If you do not receive a response, check if it would be okay to start with one hand touching the other.
- Does the receiving area already know what quality of touch it wants? Touch can be moving or still, brief or sustained, light or heavy, given with a tense or relaxed hand, coming from the whole palm or the tip of a finger.
- What is your intention while touching? Aim for kind, listening touch.
- Start with a brief touch. When you stop touching, do you sense the area wanting more, or did it feel like enough, or too much?
- Does the area respond differently to different qualities of touch?
- When you feel done with touching this area, check if another area would like touch, and if it feels okay to continue.
- Afterwards, take some time to sense any continuing reactions.

Experimenting with touch might bring a mix of emotions. You might feel comforted and soothed. You might feel angry or lonely about doing the exercise alone. You might feel frustrated or embarrassed by your responses to touch. You might feel old emotions that were stored in that part of your body, such as fear, numbness, or emptiness.

Acknowledge each response. During and after this exercise (or anytime), you can stay more present with yourself and offer a safe healing space for traumatized younger parts by acknowledging each emotion and response that arises.

"I sense something in me that feels calmer

and I sense something in me that feels angry

and I sense something in me that hates this exercise

and I sense something in me that is curious

and I sense something in me that feels young and alone

and I sense something in me that doesn't want to bother with consent.

All are here and I am the space that contains them all."*

You can turn toward each part or response with interested curiosity and sense more about it. For example, a part that does not want to bother with consent might reveal impatience, and frustration, and a sense of not deserving to be heard. With a lot of gentle listening and acknowledgment, it might reveal that it is afraid of being punished for having boundaries, and eventually soften into relief and clarity about what kind of touch is and is not okay.

Your Inner Critic might have a lot to say around touch. You can acknowledge it and what it says, without believing that it is true. You can check if it is feeling worried, perhaps about being alone and uncared-for.

Touch from others. You can try this exercise with another person supporting you to stay present but not participating with touch. You can also try exchanging touch with someone in this mindful way. Their presence will add layers of responses, for example feeling judged or wanting to manage

---

* Phrasing suggested by Ann Weiser Cornell and Barbara McGavin as part of Untangling®.

their emotions.

While our unmet needs feel as urgent as they did for an infant, we have more options as adults. We can bear witness and grieve for how painful it was and is when our needs go unmet. We can meet some old needs with our adult presence. We can notice when the outside world gives us little bits of what we need.

Keep company. With insecure attachment, our emotions and reactions around touch can be raw, wordless, and overwhelming, arising from our painful earliest experiences. When we can take a tiny step back to make space for each response and get to know it individually, we can keep ourselves company in those difficult places. With our warm adult presence, the hurt places gradually change and heal.

Find Calm: Practice Rest and Regulation

Our early experiences help our bodies learn about safety, rest, and regulation. When a baby receives enough responsive, attuned care with abundant touch, their nervous system practices moving smoothly from agitation to calm. When they spend time in calm, balanced states, they can find those states more easily in the future.

Missing calm. When a baby or young child does not receive enough responsive care, they experience developmental trauma, where the nervous system develops to handle ongoing distress rather than ongoing calm. If care is simply missing, the baby reaches out with increasing desperation, and eventually withdraws into quiet despair. The quiet shutdown is caused by strong signals (high tone) on the dorsal vagal nerves.* The nervous system becomes accustomed to that state and becomes more likely to shut down in the future.

When babies experiences active harm, especially from the same people who should be providing attuned care, their nervous system is overwhelmed with terror. They need to reach toward people for help managing the terror, but those are the same people causing harm. The urgent impulse to find safety is in direct conflict with the urgent impulse to avoid danger. The sympathetic nervous system (fight or flight) remains chronically active, rather than settling back

---

* See "Find Calm: A Polyvagal Primer" on page 150 for details about the structure of the nervous system.

to calm.

Find rest and regulation. Even if we missed out on learning how to be calm as babies, it is not too late for our nervous systems to learn about rest and regulation as adults. Kathy Kain develops and teaches simple techniques to help nervous systems reorganize and heal from developmental trauma.*

Relational trauma. Developmental trauma is inherently relational, which makes it exquisitely difficult to ask for and accept help from other people. At the same time, the need for contact and attunement is still there. When we have an attachment bond with a person or pet, physical contact with them helps our system regulate and feel safe. When we lack those bonds, we naturally struggle more with regulation and rest.

You can practice these techniques on your own or with a gentle friend. Either way, they might bring up unexpected emotions about giving and receiving support. Practice a little at a time, and remember that your responses make sense.

Settle the adrenals. The adrenals, located on top of the kidneys, are a major part of the sympathetic nervous system. It is hard to feel calm if your adrenals keep putting out stress hormones. You can help them settle and regulate your system by offering gentle touch to the kidney area, one side at a time.

As receiver, sit or lie comfortably on your back. The kidneys are mostly inside the bottom of the rib cage near the spine on each side, tipped at an angle (see figure, next page). They can curl tight against the spine, or be more open and relaxed. One kidney tends to be dominant, so one side may respond more strongly than the other.

---

* *Nurturing Resilience*, North Atlantic Books, 2018, by Kathy L. Kain and Stephen J. Terrell.

5: Intricate Body

The giver slides a slightly cupped hand under the back, starting at the waist and moving in toward the spine at an angle, touching the lowest ribs on one side. If you are working on yourself, you can use the back of your hand, lie across a rolled up towel, or imagine the contact. Find the general area, and ask the receiver if they are comfortable.

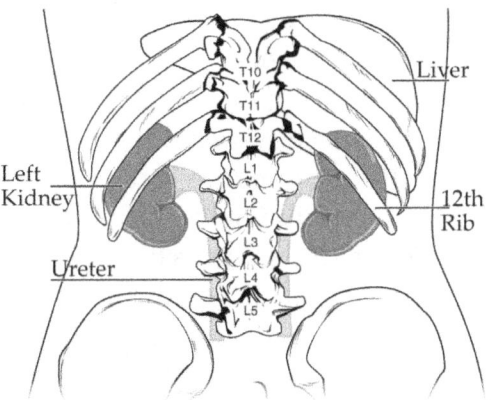

Kidneys with ribs, back view

Friendly, attentive contact. The giver simply offers friendly, attentive contact, without demanding or expecting any specific result. Stay in contact for five to fifteen minutes, or until the receiver (or giver) wants to stop or switch sides.

You might feel confused or uncertain as you search for a state that is new to you. You might feel a sense of warmth and relaxation. You might feel a stronger pulse in the area as the kidney allows more blood to flow through it. You might feel several waves of activation and settling, tensing and relaxing. You might feel relief in spacious support to find calm.

Practice rest. Healing from trauma can be framed as a quest for safety. At first, people in recovery often focus on detecting and eliminating threats. Traumatized people also need to learn or remember how to feel safe inside themselves.

Someone who experienced developmental trauma may alternate between agitation and shutdown, without true rest. The sympathetic nervous system stays active until it is overridden by a strong signal on the dorsal vagal nerves, creating shutdown.

Kathy Kain points out that a milder signal (low tone) on the dorsal vagal system promotes digestion, immune function, cell repair, and reduction of inflammation. This rest state is crucially important in avoiding and healing from chronic health conditions that often affect trauma survivors, as shown by the ACE study.*

When you practice low tone dorsal vagal rest, you practice the visceral experience of feeling safe. Your body can turn inward and repair, because nothing in the external environment requires your attention. You might have memories of safety to draw on, or you might be seeking an experience that is new to you.

Sit or lie down in a place where it feels okay to experiment with safety. Do everything you can to get physically comfortable, including turning down the lights if that helps. You might want someone to sit with you, perhaps gently supporting a kidney as described earlier, or you might prefer to be alone.

If you have a time limit, give yourself enough time at the end to transition back to full wakefulness. You can keep the experiment short to start, perhaps ten minutes of resting and five minutes of transition.

Simply be. You want to find a state that is in between the activation of the sympathetic nervous system and the dissociation or freeze of strong dorsal vagal activity. You do

---

* "Relationship of Childhood Abuse and Household Dysfunction to Many of the Leading Causes of Death in Adults. The Adverse Childhood Experiences (ACE) Study." Felitti, Vincent J. et al., American Journal of Preventive Medicine, Volume 14, Issue 4, 245-258. https://ajpmonline.org/article/S0749-3797(98)00017-8/pdf

not have to do anything here. All expectations and pressure are removed. You do not have to manage yourself or your relationship with anyone else. You do not have to respond. You are off duty. You can simply be.

You might feel like you are drifting, or starting to fall asleep, or falling into yourself. You might feel your mind chattering along, refusing to relax. You might notice specific physical tensions more strongly. You might notice how hard you work all the time. You could let your mind and your body know that you hear them. Whatever happens is part of the process of finding your way into rest somewhere in the middle between activation and freeze.

Permission not to rest. If you tend to work hard at everything, including resting, you might let yourself off the hook by giving yourself permission not to rest. Part of feeling safe is being okay exactly the way you are in this moment. Move in the direction of relief, whatever that means for you. Perhaps you want to change position, or ask your companion to move farther away or not look at you. Perhaps you want to talk about what you are noticing. Invite your system to move toward rest, and let it tell you what it needs along the way.

Your body makes sense. Your body and nervous system are doing their best to survive and thrive. If they were shaped by traumatic conditions, it takes time to adapt to safer circumstances. People often feel intense shame about difficulties with attachment, regulation, and rest. It is easier to find calm when you can warmly allow your body to react just the way it does.

Find Calm: A Polyvagal Primer

When we understand how our nervous system is put together, we can work with the body to find calm after being traumatized, rather than fighting with the barriers we encounter.

Stephen Porges has done decades of careful research into the parts of the nervous system that control activation and settling: the sympathetic and parasympathetic nervous systems, which together make up the autonomic nervous system.* He found that the parasympathetic system has two parts, creating a hierarchy of three systems that respond to danger and also function in safety.

Action: sympathetic nervous system. The sympathetic nervous system helps you take action. It powers fight-or-flight reactions, as well as any muscular effort such as standing and walking. It raises your heart rate and breathing rate, increases blood flow to large muscles, and dilates the pupils of the eyes. To balance this use of energy and resources, blood flow decreases to digestive organs, and immune system function decreases.

The sympathetic nervous system is activated by hormones secreted by the adrenals, located on top of the kidneys. Once the hormones are circulating, it takes a few minutes for them to clear from the body, which is why an adrenaline rush does not instantly subside, even when we realize there is no

---

* *The Polyvagal Theory*, W. W. Norton & Company, 2011, by Stephen W. Porges.

5: Intricate Body

danger or the danger is over.

Rest: parasympathetic nervous system. The parasympathetic nervous system helps you rest, digest, and repair. It decreases your heart rate and breathing rate, increases blood flow to digestive organs, and increases immune system function.

Did you ever wonder how someone with a paralyzing spinal cord injury can still breathe and digest food? While sympathetic nerves originate from the spinal cord at the middle and lower spine, parasympathetic nerves originate directly from the brain. Parasympathetic nerves are also called vagus ("wandering") nerves, or the tenth cranial nerves.

Many vagus nerve fibers. The Polyvagal Theory says that there are older and newer parts of the vagus nerves, which are the long nerves that run directly from the brain stem to heart, lungs, and digestive organs. The older and newer fibers combine on each side to form a right vagus nerve and left vagus nerve. They have slightly different functions on each side since we are not fully symmetrical. The nerves have afferent (sensory, toward the brain) fibers and efferent (motor, from the brain) fibers, creating feedback loops that regulate the organs and keep them functioning in their ideal range.

Older: dorsal vagus. The dorsal (back) vagal nerve fibers start at the back of the brain stem. They are unmyelinated (unsheathed) and thus send relatively slow and imprecise signals. A strong signal (known as high tone) on these nerve fibers causes heart and breathing to slow dramatically. The body goes limp and freezes, or "plays dead." This is different from a tense "must do!"/"can't do!" freeze caused by conflicting impulses.

We share this ancient system with all vertebrates. For

reptiles, slow heart and breathing allow them to dive underwater for longer periods and to survive a predator's interest. For mammals, whose brains require more oxygen, a dorsal vagal freeze can be fatal if it goes on too long.

The nervous system resorts to the dorsal vagal freeze when it evaluates that it is our only hope for survival, or when it has given up on survival. It is completely involuntary and not a cause for shame or self-recrimination for "not fighting back."

Dorsal rest. A less strong signal (low tone) on the dorsal vagus nerve fibers coordinates digestion, immune response, and cell repair. The body goes into this important rest state when we feel safe and there are no demands on us.

If we experienced early developmental trauma, our nervous system might not have learned how to access this state. If we have PTSD from shock trauma, we might remain too vigilant to rest deeply. This leads to chronic issues with digestion, immune response, and fatigue.

Newer: ventral vagus. The ventral (front) vagal nerve fibers start at the front of the brain stem. They are myelinated (sheathed) and thus send fast, precise signals. All mammals have this system, which evolved to help mammals get the dependable high oxygen levels we need, as well as conserve energy when we are at rest.

Vagal brake on heart rate. The human heart has a pacemaker that beats around 100 times per minute. A strong signal on the ventral fibers of the vagus nerve slows the pacemaker, acting as a brake on the heart rate. Since ventral vagus signals are fast and precise, the vagal brake can be adjusted nearly instantaneously to slow or speed the heart as needed.

When we sit and chat with someone, the vagal brake slows the heart because we need less blood flow to muscles. When we stand up, we need more blood flow to support movement. The vagal brake releases, allowing our heart to beat faster without adrenal hormones.

The ventral vagus fibers help initiate each inhalation (in-breath). Exhalations (out-breaths) happen without effort as the diaphragm relaxes. During the inhalation signal, the vagal brake signal to the heart is interrupted, and the heart speeds up a little bit. This difference in heart rate between inhalation and exhalation is known as Respiratory Sinus Arrhythmia*, or RSA. It is used in medical experiments to measure the strength of the ventral vagal signal noninvasively, mostly in children where RSA is more pronounced.

Social engagement. The higher the ventral vagal tone, the more pronounced the RSA difference becomes. Higher ventral vagal tone is better, leading to a lower resting heart rate, healthier digestion, and more energy available for social engagement and attachment bonds.

The ventral vagus fibers originate in the same area of the brain stem as nerves controlling facial expressions, speech, singing, and swallowing. They coordinate our social engagement: using our avenue of expression to talk with and respond to other people. They sensitively detect friendly or threatening behavior, and adjust the vagal brake as necessary. When we feel safe, our heart rate slows, and when we feel threatened, it speeds up.

Release your ears. The ventral vagus nerve fibers also

---

* Respiratory (breathing) Sinus Arrhythmia (lack of rhythm) gets "Sinus" from the sinoatrial node of the heart, which is the heart's pacemaker. "Atrial" comes from the atrium, one of the sections of the heart. "Sino" comes from the sinus venarum, a cavity (sinus means open space or cavity) that exists in the embryonic heart, becoming part of the atrial wall after birth. The sinoatrial node is in that part of the wall of the right atrium in the heart.

interact with our hearing. They tighten the muscles of the middle ear, tuning it toward higher conversational pitches rather than the lower pitch of a predator's roar. If we grew up in an abusive environment where humans were the source of danger, we might unconsciously tighten our middle ear all the time, straining to hear approaching voices that signal danger.

Try asking your middle ears on both sides to relax. Even if you do not know how to contact them with precision, you might notice a release in your jaw and maybe even your shoulders.

Breath supports calm. Stephen Porges points out that playing a wind instrument makes ideal contact with the ventral vagus: a slow controlled exhalation, attention to facial muscles to maintain embouchure, and engagement with others when playing in a group or for an audience. Singing does the same thing.

To calm your system, take a quick breath in, then blow out gently for as long as the breath lasts. Try it a few times and see if your heart rate slows down.

No wonder. When we understand the underlying structure of our nervous system, we can make sense of our behavior more easily. No wonder it was hard to make small talk when we were already frightened. No wonder we find it hard to rest if we never got a chance to feel safe when our nervous system was developing. No wonder we got still and quiet when we thought there was no way out. Our nervous system is doing its best to help us survive. We can help it learn new patterns that serve us better in the present.

Get to Know Your Guts

The vagus nerves connect our brain and gut. As we learn more about both, we can invite them to relax and work better together.

Our belly could be a source of warmth, inner connection, and flow. Our gut feelings could guide us on when to move forward and when to back away. All too often, trauma disconnects us from our inner core. Our belly tightens against pain, fear, and misery rather than relaxing into pleasure and comfort.

For many of us, our belly is a mysterious mass of unknown organs, often the source of uncomfortable sensations and emotions that we avoid. We can begin to reconnect through kind touch and specific knowledge about the organs inside.

Soft hands. As you explore your belly, keep your hands soft and open. You can sense more and go deeper if you approach with kindness than if you poke or push hard. Go slowly, and respect any barriers or resistance you encounter. If it is not comfortable to touch your belly, you can imagine the touch instead, or sense your organs from the inside.

If you lie down for these explorations, bend your knees to give your abdominal muscles some slack and allow them to relax.

Bring your hands gently to your belly. Listen to the sensations both in your hands and in your belly. Make space for any judgments, emotions, or stories that come up as you listen.

Find landmarks. Your abdomen is the lower part of your torso from diaphragm to pelvis. With soft hands, find your lower ribs along the sides of your body, hard ridges with gaps between them. Follow their lower curve around to the front and feel the space between them, below the bottom of your sternum (breastbone).

Now find your rounded pelvic bones ("hip bones") at your sides below your waist and follow their curve around to the front. Also touch your navel (belly button), about halfway between your pelvis and ribs.

Motility. In addition to sliding and shifting with the breath and other body movements, organs have intrinsic motility: a gentle swell and deflation four to five times per minute, as described by Jean-Pierre Barral.* Motility can also mean the waves of contraction that move food through the digestive system. This is a different use of the same word.

In general, organs swell away from the body's midline and deflate back toward it. You can sense motility by letting your hand connect with an organ and feeling for subtle movement. An organ's motility can be restricted by tension or adhesions. If you do not feel movement, gently suggesting movement and amplifying what you feel can loosen restrictions and help the organ move more freely. Remember to soften your hands, and believe your subtle sensations.

As you visit individual organs, notice how easy or difficult it is to connect with them. How do the organs respond when you offer contact? Are there any specific emotions or stories associated with each one?

Large liver. Your liver is a large solid three-dimensional wedge under your lower ribs on your right side. The narrow

---

* *Visceral Manipulation*, Eastland Press, 2005, by Jean-Pierre Barral and Pierre Mercier.

5: Intricate Body

part of the wedge extends across the left side under the diaphragm, overlapping with the stomach. The liver is deep and broad, filling your upper right abdomen from front to back. See the large divided triangle at the top of the figure.

The liver produces bile to digest fats, breaks down toxins in the blood, and synthesizes required proteins, among other functions. It is our largest internal organ.

Put a gentle hand across your right lower ribs and check for your liver's motility, swelling slightly toward the right side of your body, and deflating back to center. Let your hand ride the faster pulse and slower breath while you sense for the quieter motility.

You can sink your attention through skin, past the bones to the organ. If you feel your body tighten or push back, try softening your hand and sensing rather than pushing.

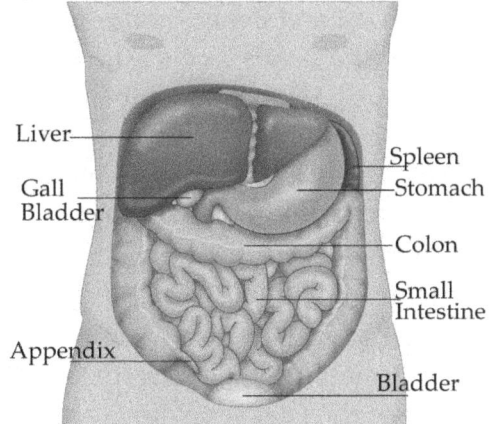

Abdominal organs

Stomach sack. Under your left lower ribs, across from the liver, the stomach is a hollow sack which grows much larger when full of food, sometimes extending below your navel. The stomach and liver overlap below your sternum. The rounded fundus of the stomach nudges up against the diaphragm, keeping the stomach from being pulled up by the esophagus. See the oval next to and under the liver in the figure.

The stomach chemically and mechanically breaks down

the food we eat into a liquid called chyme.

Sense for the liver's motility with one hand, and then sense the stomach swelling to your left with the other hand just below your lower left ribs. Gently encourage the stomach and liver to move away and together in sync, like dance partners.

Folded small intestine. From the stomach, partly-digested food exits into the duodenum, a semi-rigid tube that curves around the pancreas (not shown). From there food goes into the jejunum and ileum (not to be confused with the ilium bones of the pelvis), which together form a long (around 4 meters, or 13 feet) soft tube folded up on itself like too many shirts crammed in a drawer. The small intestine fills the space below the liver and stomach. See the smaller folded tube in the figure, previous page.

The three parts of the small intestine absorb water and nutrients from the food we eat.

Place one or both hands near your navel to sense small intestine motility, which is a circling expansion up and rightward, and then deflation down and leftward. You might also feel the rumbles of digestion.

Spacious large intestine. The small intestine connects to the large intestine at the ileocecal valve, slightly above and to the right of the navel. The large intestine (or colon) is a wider tube running along the edges of the area filled by the small intestine with three relatively straight segments and a fourth curved one: the ascending colon on the far right, the transverse colon running just under the liver and stomach, and the descending colon on the far left. The sigmoid colon makes the final curvy connection to the anus behind the bladder. See the larger tube surrounding the small intestine in the figure, previous page.

The large intestine extracts remaining water and salt from digested food and excretes waste via the anus. It hosts up to 100 trillion symbiotic microbes that help with fiber digestion and produce vitamins and intestinal gas.

Place one hand on your lower right side toward the front and the other hand on your lower left side toward the back to sense large intestine motility. It has a circular motion similar to the small intestine, expanding along its path toward the ileocecal valve, and then deflating back toward the sigmoid colon.

Nourishing mesentery. The intestines are living tissues that need a blood supply and a way to transfer out digested nutrients. Rather than running along the tube, blood vessels nourish every part of the intestines from a fan-folded sheet of tissue called the mesentery. The mesentery attaches to the back of the abdomen on the right side on a surprisingly short (15 centimeters, or 6 inches) diagonal line called the mesenteric root and fans out from there to the whole small and large intestine.

Rest and digest. How does your belly feel now, after some gentle contact with specific organs? Has your sense of your belly as a whole changed?

Our digestive system is crucial to our long-term health. When our sympathetic nervous system (fight or flight) is constantly active, our parasympathetic nervous system (rest and digest) is less active and digestion slows down. Our guts and our nervous system can help calm each other, helping us feel better overall.

Self-Care for Sticky Lungs

The domed diaphragm divides our torso, with digestive organs below it and lungs above. We can sense our lungs and encourage repair after illness or injury.

Healthy breathing is a relaxed symphony of movement. On inhalation, the diaphragm widens and flattens downward. Each rib traces an arc up and out like a bucket handle. The spine gathers to support the ribs. The lungs, anchored at the top near the collarbones, extend easily along the chest walls to fill the increased space, pulling in a fresh breath.

On exhalation, the diaphragm releases back into a dome. The ribs return down and in. The spine lengthens. The lungs slide back up to their initial position, expelling air.*

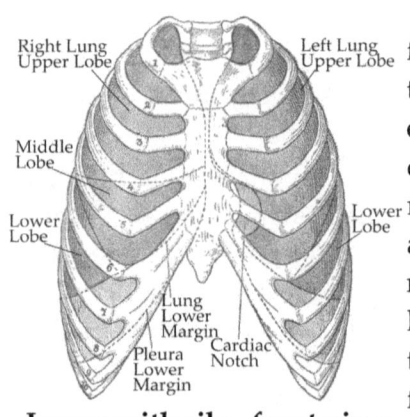

Lungs with ribs, front view

Lung structure. The lungs fill the full thickness of the torso from front to back, and extend from collarbones to diaphragm, whose dome rises as high as the sixth rib and the bottom of the sternum. The lungs have three lobes on the right and only two on the left to make room for the heart (see figure).

In a growing embryo, the

---

* Brief MRI video of breathing from Tatiana Kuzhelkova. https://youtu.be/u-O8CgkCW1I

intestines and stomach develop first. The esophagus (food tube) grows up from the stomach, and then turns back down to become the trachea (windpipe). At the level of the fourth ribs, the trachea divides to become the two bronchi to the lungs, which divide again to become the secondary bronchi that enter each lobe, and then continue dividing to develop into the tiny bronchioles and alveoli where oxygen exchange occurs. Blood vessels and nerves grow in tandem with the developing bronchial tree. See figure "Respiratory system" on page 167.

Slippery membranes. The inner chest wall is coated with a membrane called the parietal pleura. The lung lobes are covered with a similar membrane called the visceral pleura. A layer of slippery interstitial fluid between the two membranes allows them to move along each other as needed.

The individual lobes can also slide along each other. This allows us to twist our torso without straining delicate lung tissue.*

Sticky adhesions. When the body repairs an injury, extra fibers might attach between adjacent membranes, creating an adhesion that locally sticks them together, restricting smooth motion. Extra fibers can also connect within tissue to create a contracture, restricting elasticity. Lung adhesions and contractures can result from an impact to the torso, or by breathing air contaminated with industrial by-products, car exhaust, tobacco smoke, forest fire smoke, or other pollutants. Adhesions can also result from acute and chronic illnesses such as bronchitis, pneumonia, Covid-19, asthma, and emphysema.

---

* Lung anatomy and treatment information from Jeffrey Burch, "Manual Therapy for Lung Rehabilitation," online class April 14 and 16, 2020.

When adhesions or contractures impede inner sliding, nerves detect the strain, and muscles tighten protectively in the area to keep lung tissue from tearing. Our "bad" posture, chronic muscular knots, or lack of flexibility might be caused by a deeper restriction.

Gentle separation. Where tissues have stuck together, we can gently encourage separation of adhesions to restore healthy movement.

Note: If you currently have or are recovering from an acute illness or injury, allow several weeks of healing before attempting to release adhesions. Your body is busy and does not need additional input. If you have a chronic condition that causes fragile bones, blood vessels, or lung tissue, such as osteoporosis, vascular Ehlers-Danlos Syndrome, or emphysema, consult your doctor and be cautious with this technique.

Get comfortable. Find a position where your torso is comfortably supported, lying down or sitting against a back rest or standing against a wall or closed door. Check in with your body's needs. Perhaps you need a drink of water or a bathroom break before continuing. Loosen tight clothing. Add pillows for support and a blanket if you feel cold.

Sense into your hands, along each finger and palm and back of the hands. Give each hand a little massage, and sense both the giving and receiving hand. Invite your hands to be warm and relaxed.

Breathe. As you settle in, bring your attention to your breathing. Observe quietly, riding along with the in-breath and out-breath. Notice where your body moves with breathing, and where it is still. Notice what feels flexible, and what feels stiff. Slowly move your attention along your front from collarbones to the bottom of your ribs, around to the sides, and along your back. Sense from the inside, and with your eyes, and with your hands resting on your body.

Relaxed touch. Let a hand move to an area over your lungs that wants attention, perhaps somewhere that feels immobile, stiff, or tender. If nothing specific calls to you, choose a place on one of your sides, since they often receive less attention than the front or back.

Let your relaxed hand sink in to contact skin, muscle, and bone, and sense for the inner chest wall and lung underneath. You can turn so your body weight pushes your ribs into your hand. For example, if you are touching your right side, turn to lie on your right side. Alternatively, you can put a weight on your hand such as a book or a yoga sandbag so it can sink in while remaining relaxed. The area you are touching might feel tender, but it should not hurt so much that you tense up. If it hurts, lighten your pressure or choose a different spot.

Breath adds movement. With your hand as an anchor, your relaxed breathing provides movement to gradually stretch and release adhesions. Ride along with your breath for a while, resting into your hand. Check that your hand is relaxed, rather than pushing or tensing.

You might feel some unwinding, where the impulse toward motion comes from the place that is releasing. Allow movement to arise from the inside, rather than imposing a stretch or pull from the outside. Allow sounds to arise as well.

Stay with this spot until you feel done, or until you get a sign of release like a deeper breath or sigh, twitches, increased movement with breathing, or a wave of emotion. It can be both a relief and a challenge to breathe more freely and take up more space. Grief and other emotions can flow more easily with more room to breathe.

When one adhesion releases, another one might become more evident. You can follow your inner sense to a new spot and repeat the process: make contact, rest your body weight over your hand, and allow your breath to add gentle movement. After three or four releases, give yourself some time to rest before getting up.

You might feel increased lightness, spaciousness, ease, and flow. You might feel sore where something is newly moving. (A bath with Epsom salts can help.) Or, it might feel like nothing much changed. Over the next few days, increased movement in one area allows other areas to work themselves free. You might notice improved mobility in your back, shoulders, or neck. You might notice that your voice is more full or has a wider range.

Time to adapt. Give your body plenty of time to adapt, and wait a couple of weeks before addressing any further adhesions. Gradual change is more comfortable and sustainable.

Let Go for More Sound

Sound is created by movement, including the movement of our lungs and breath. We can be quieter by using less effort to create less motion, or by adding the effort of restraint. When our voice is open and free, we can choose a sound level from relaxed silence to barely audible to resoundingly loud.

Small children shriek happily, or ask embarrassing questions in their carrying voices, effortlessly far louder than the adults around them would prefer. Adults plead with them to use their inside voices. Children gradually learn a quieter register.

If our voice was met with scorn, or threats, or indifference, we might battle bands of constraining tension to make sound. When we are tasked with keeping secrets, we tighten around our voice to keep the truth from slipping out. Unresolved fear can constrict our whole body, trying to stay small and unnoticed.

Accurate map. We might want to sing in a choir, or share our perspective in a meeting, or express a boundary, or speak up against injustice. To restore our ability to speak or sing loudly and clearly, we need to restore our ease of movement. When we map our bodies accurately, we learn which muscles need to work and which do not to produce sound.

We tighten around the need to keep parts of ourselves hidden. As we restore our ease of movement, we also restore our ability to be our complete selves. The more we bring frozen parts into present safety and reduce ongoing threats in our lives, the more we can be available for relaxed movement rather than being continually tensed to fight or flee.

Balanced and buoyant. Ongoing tension might curl us forward protectively, or pull us back in a show of size and strength. Ease of movement comes from balance and buoyancy rather than a fixed posture or alignment. As we get to know our bodies, we have more choices about how we sit and stand and move.

Our voice is supported by resilient springiness in our feet, knees, and hips. A relaxed pelvis supports the spine rising through the center of the body in gentle flexible weight-bearing curves. Take some time to sense your legs. If you sense tension or contraction, offer the tense area warm support and invite it to release.

You can find a neutral, buoyant relationship between your torso and hips by lying on the floor with your knees bent and feet on the floor. As your body takes in the floor's support, sense for tension or pulling and invite it to ease. Can you find a similar ease while standing? Walking slowly backward might help bring awareness to habitual tension that is no longer needed.

Poised head. Our heavy head balances on top of the cervical spine, supported from the center. The atlanto-occipital (neck-skull) joint is between our ears, at the level of the roof of the mouth. The jaw attaches to the skull at both sides and hangs lower than the joint between skull and neck.

You can find the joint between your skull and neck by rocking your head slightly back and forth on the top of your neck, letting your chin jut forward and back. If you run your tongue back along the roof of your mouth, it points to the joint. When your head balances easily on your neck, the surrounding muscles can release. Do you sense pulling or compression along the back of your neck? Invite it to lengthen. Does that allow your chin to drop and your head to float more comfortably?

Breathe easy. The lungs fill the top half of the torso. Air flows only into your lungs, not into your belly.

The whole torso responds to the breath. During inhalation, the diaphragm pushes down the abdominal organs, which push down the muscles of the pelvic diaphragm. The intercostal muscles between the ribs pull the ribs up and out like bucket handles. The sternum moves out and the spine compresses slightly as the lungs fill with air.

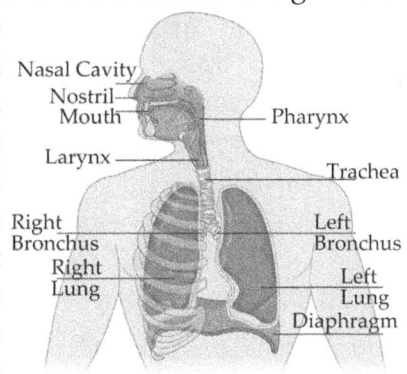

Respiratory system

During exhalation the diaphragm relaxes its pressure on the abdomen, the ribs move down and in, and the spine releases to its full length.

Air flows in. The mouth, jaw, neck, and throat do not need to work to bring air in. The air simply flows through the mouth or nose, down the trachea (windpipe), and into the lungs, filling them from the top down. Invite your mouth and neck to rest while you sense where you feel the movement of your breath.

The trachea has rings of cartilage that keep it open to the diameter of a quarter. You can gently touch its ridges in the notch just above your sternum (breastbone). The esophagus (food tube) is a flat muscular tube behind the trachea against the cervical spine. It only expands when food is moving through it. The mouth and throat muscles work to swallow food, but not to breathe.

Pronunciation is movement. We make sound with our out-breath as it moves through our vocal folds (also called vocal cords), causing them to vibrate. We control pitch and volume with the small muscles around the larynx (voice box) in the throat.

Articulation (speech) is separate from phonation (creating sound). Each speech sound in every language is made with different movements of muscular lips, mouth, and tongue.

On a steady pitch, say the pure vowels: "ah, eh, ee, oh, ooh." Sense how your larynx stays steady as your mouth moves to shape the vowels. Now change pitch up and down while saying "ah" and feel your larynx change while your mouth stays steady. Say "that" and feel your tongue move from your teeth to the roof of your mouth.

Full sound. Either sitting or standing, take some time to invite your body into balance. Scan for unneeded tension and invite it to release. Imagine saying "hello," and notice which muscles prepare to work. Are all of them needed to make sound? Now say "hello" out loud. Listen for resonance and sense for ease.

As you speak or sing throughout your day, sense how much work your body is doing. Look for safe opportunities to feel your full size, move with ease, and let your sound take up space.

Look into the Present

Chronic muscle tension from past trauma and present threats affects the eyes along with the rest of the body. Our eyes are directly involved in orienting to danger and can hold incomplete trauma responses.

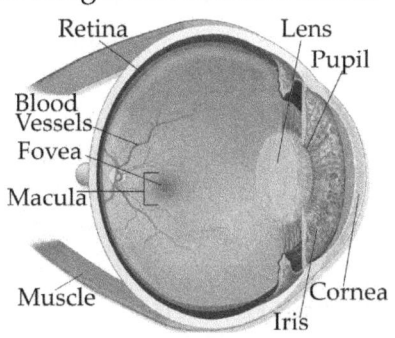

Eye looking to the right

Light enters the eye through the pupil and is focused by the lens onto the retina in the back of the eye. Muscles in and around the eye control where we look, whether we have depth perception, how much light enters the eye, and how clearly we see. Chronic muscle tension can affect all those functions.

External eye muscles. Six muscles around the outside of each eye move it up, down, side to side, and rotate it. Two muscles are shown in the figure. An imbalance in these muscles can lead to strabismus (crossed eyes) where the eyes do not track together, which interrupts depth perception and can cause double vision. These muscles can also pull the eye out of shape, leading to blurred vision because incoming light is not focused accurately on the retina at the back of the eye.

Clear vision also depends on saccades, small fast involuntary eye movements that scan what we want to see. The retina has a small high-resolution area, the macula, containing an even smaller highest-resolution area, the fovea. Saccades allow the fovea to take in more of what we look at, building up a sharp image. We can support sharp vision by noticing details, allowing our eyes to move from one detail to the next.

Internal eye muscles. Small muscles inside the eye change the shape of the lens to focus on near objects. This is called accommodation. Ongoing stress and tension make accommodation more difficult. We can let those muscles rest by looking into the distance as a break from close work such as looking at a computer.

The iris contains tiny muscles that expand and contract the pupil depending on the amount of light available. We can keep these muscles active through their full range by spending time in bright sunlight as well as walking around in a (safe) dark environment.

Neck and head. Our neck muscles are also involved in vision. Our eyes want our head to move smoothly to direct our gaze, and neck tension gets in the way. Watch a dog out on a walk sometime. The head swings easily and eagerly in the direction of each object that catches the dog's attention. We can practice allowing our head to follow our gaze as our eyes wander toward what interests us, nearby and in the distance.

Full field of vision. In Emergency Mode during or after trauma, our field of vision narrows to take in only what is right in front of us. Everything else can wait until the emergency is over. When we do regain a sense of safety, we might suddenly notice decorations or other details in our environment that have been there all along.

You can invite your field of vision to broaden by waving

your hands at the periphery of your vision while continuing to look forward. You can also consciously circle through your full field of vision. Without moving your head, move your eyes to look up, around to the left, down, around to the right, and back up. Circle the other way too.

Trauma can affect our desire to see clearly. We might have been punished for seeing abuse, or experienced gaslighting: "This isn't happening. You don't see it." Our eyes might blur, cross, or reflexively avoid the direction that brought danger.

Boundary bubble repair. Someone injured from the upper left might experience reinjury because they do not see obstacles in that area. Our sense of a boundary bubble around us feels torn or has a hole. We can repair the boundary bubble by checking which directions feel safe, and which directions feel more dangerous or threatening. We can gently pay attention to the border between a safe area and a dangerous area to help the boundary bubble heal there.

Orient to danger. Our eyes and neck might be affected because of an incomplete orienting response. The nervous system wants enough time to sense danger, orient toward it by turning the head and focusing the senses, and then respond. When a traumatic event happens too fast, or during sleep, the incomplete orienting response can leave lingering tension.

Somatic Experiencing® includes techniques for releasing incomplete responses by attending to bodily reactions while gradually and gently revisiting the traumatic event. In a slowed-down version of the event, we can invite the neck, head, and eyes to move as they wish to orient toward the source of danger. Release reactions might include twitches, warmth, deep breaths, belly sounds, or tears.

Rest your eyes. We can allow our eyes to rest and invite them to release tension by palming: briefly rub your hands together to warm them, and then rest the palms over the eyes, touching the bony sockets, but not the eyes themselves. Allow the closed eyes to rest into darkness.

Note: Palming is not recommended for people diagnosed with glaucoma because it can raise the internal eye pressure.

Palm for as long as it feels good, anywhere from a few seconds to many minutes. In his book *Vision for Life*, Meir Schneider recommends several shorter sessions throughout the day rather than one longer session.* Either way can be beneficial. Palming can be restful after driving, computer use, or any other visually intensive activity.

If palming is uncomfortable, or in addition to palming, you can invite your eyes to fall back into your skull. We unconsciously tense our muscles to look out at the world, and forget to relax again. Let light come to you rather than reaching for it. You might feel your face, jaw, and even shoulders let go. Your fingertips can give gentle pressure to the bony sockets around the eyes to help you sense into that area.

Clarity in the present. Many of these tips can be done while walking, waiting in line, or any time we have a few moments in our day. As we look into the distance, notice details, move our eyes through their full range of motion, or let them sink back in their sockets, we connect with our present sensory experience. Practicing rest and kindness toward our eyes gradually eases habits of chronic tension. As we look at the world with more relaxation and clarity, we see more of the beauty and safety available to us.

When we understand our insides, we can sense ourselves more accurately and move in the world more confidently.

---

* *Vision for Life*, North Atlantic Books, 2016, by Meir Schneider.

Resources

The Polyvagal Theory, W. W. Norton & Company, 2011, by Stephen W. Porges is a dense compilation of his research papers in technical medical language.

Nurturing Resilience, North Atlantic Books, 2018, by Kathy L. Kain and Stephen J. Terrell has detailed information about developmental trauma and what can help

A Pathway to Health, North Atlantic Books, 2010, by Alison Harvey is a friendly introduction to Visceral Manipulation bodywork, including client stories.

Visceral Manipulation, Eastland Press, 2005, by Jean-Pierre Barral and Pierre Mercier describes Visceral Manipulation bodywork in technical medical language.

What Every Singer Needs to Know About the Body, Plural Publishing, 2012, by Melissa Malde, MaryJean Allen, and Kurt-Alexander Zeller, has anatomy and exercises to sing better.

The Structures and Movement of Breathing, Gia Publications, 2001, by Barbara Conable, contains accurate anatomy for singers.

Vision for Life, North Atlantic Books, 2016, by Meir Schneider contains his story of healing from legal blindness with the Bates Method, and his carefully described exercises to improve vision.

Fixing My Gaze, Basic Books, 2009, by neuroscientist Susan R. Barry describes her recovery of stereoscopic (3D) vision after a lifetime of crossed eyes. It includes information about the neurology of vision, specifics about vision therapy, and the far reaching effects of seeing depth.

Embodying Hope

6: Relationship Skills

Relationships can be both our best support and our biggest challenge. With a nervous system already wounded by past trauma, navigating connections with strangers, friends, and family becomes even harder.

Relationships require skills and practice, like learning to play a musical instrument. They can be hard work, but they should not be hard in the sense of painfully grinding us down. The goal is for everyone to feel safe and nourished.

We build our skills patiently. We find the boundaries where we end and others begin. We learn to listen and speak with clarity and kindness. We share feedback and resolve conflict. We acknowledge power and privilege. We offer and receive support. We embody the culture of kindness we always wanted and hoped for.

Intervene for a Better World

Be kind, for everyone is fighting a hard battle.
—Ian MacLaren

The dearest hope of many survivors is to fit in smoothly with society, to look and act "normal." We want to interact with other people skillfully. We want to be liked. We want to be heard. We want to give and receive courtesy and consideration as part of a supportive community.

Narrow window of tolerance. An irritated nervous system makes it harder to interact with people in a kind way. It narrows our window of tolerance for stressful events. For example, when feeling calm and happy, you might shrug if someone accidentally stepped on your toe, whereas in a less settled state you might snarl, "Watch where you're going!"

If the toe-stepper also had a difficult day, they might respond poorly to being snarled at, resulting in conflict that neither of you wanted.

Social anxiety. Many abuse survivors have social anxiety. When the people around us have been a source of harm rather than comfort, we focus on learning how to avoid abuse rather than how to interact in positive ways. It makes sense to feel overwhelmed by people and the intricacies of dealing with them, both individually and in large groups.

In Emergency Mode, our brains continue to focus on danger rather than connection. Not only did survivors miss learning tools for skillful interaction in the past, but it is physiologically more difficult to read social signals and respond appropriately while terrified in the present.

Imperfectly nice. Victim-blaming puts additional pressure on survivors to stay eternally on guard to avoid "causing" or "inviting" abuse. While clearer boundaries can discourage abusive or predatory behavior, we are not responsible for magically preventing abuse. It is the person committing abuse who is responsible for it.

At the same time, survivors are blamed for pushing people away and (for those seen as women) socially penalized for having clear boundaries and not being nice enough. The fine line between "not nice enough" and "too nice" can be impossible to find.

When to intervene. For all these reasons, survivors tend to be very aware of public rules and try hard to follow them. It can be both confusing and irritating when others casually break rules, especially when it involves harm to shared resources.

On the one hand, social rules say, "Mind your own business. Don't interfere." On the other hand, silence gives tacit approval to oblivious behavior we witness. We each have to decide when to resist by saying something, and when to let it go. We might have a strong sense of responsibility to make the world a better place by speaking up, and we might also have limits in our skills and inner resources.

Harassment, bullying, and abuse are even more difficult to address in the moment than breaking smaller social rules. Survivors might freeze or have other strong reactions that interfere with finding a skillful response. Looking toward the victim with compassion can make a difference in itself.

Consider privilege. Those of us with more privilege tend to benefit from social rules and feel entitled to enforce them on others. Less privileged people are more limited by social rules and punished more harshly for breaking them. For example, a Black person risks being stopped and possibly arrested for walking through a restricted area, where a white person could slide by with a smile and a wave. We need to be careful not to reinforce privilege and oppression with our interventions.

Assume good intent. When we cut across a lawn where it says, "Do not walk on the grass," we are doing it because we did not see the sign, or the path is blocked, or we really need the shortcut right now. When we see someone else cut across the same lawn, we tend to assume they do not care about the grass.

When we intervene, we can start by assuming that the person means well and is doing their best. They know more about their situation than we do, and they are doing what makes sense for them in the moment.

No dogs. On a rainy morning walk, I was surprised to see a white couple throwing balls for their large dogs inside the tennis courts. I decided to intervene by saying, "The dog park is up the hill," and pointing. They responded by saying, "It's too muddy up there." Astonished, I said, "It's rude to run the dogs where they'll damage the special surface on the courts." They responded angrily, and did not change their behavior. I confirmed later that a sign at the entrance to the courts says, "No dogs."

I started with the positive assumption that they mistook the fenced courts for the dog park. In this case it turned out they felt unhealthy entitlement to use the courts in a way that damages them for everyone else. I do not know if my intervention changed their behavior in the future, or whether phrasing it differently would have worked better.

At least they know that someone sees them misusing the tennis courts.

Feelings and needs. Robyn Posin suggests a long form intervention that includes feelings and needs: "Excuse me, I know this may feel intrusive and perhaps rude, but it really upsets me to see people (fill in the blank) because (fill in the blank). And, I try to speak up about things like this, just in case the person involved might simply not have considered the impact of (doing whatever it is) on the (whatever)..."*

Missing information. A shorter form imparts possibly missing information and gives people room to figure out what they need to do for themselves. "The dog park is up there."

Thanks. When a stranger approaches us about a rule we are breaking, we might feel startled and upset even if they do it kindly. We are likely to respond defensively in the moment even if we think it over later and decide they might be right.

We could assume they mean well and thank them for the information. If they have not given thought to privilege and oppression and it is one microaggression too many, we might react angrily.

Thoughtful interventions. Interacting with strangers can be difficult at the best of times. When we want to intervene with a criticism or correction, we can pause to consider whether an intervention is needed and find kind phrasing for our reminder. As our nervous system heals over time, our window of tolerance widens for minor infractions, and we can intervene more calmly and skillfully for larger issues.

---

* Private communication, April 4, 2019, quoted with permission.

Kindness, Not Contempt

Contempt is regarding something or someone as inferior, vile, or worthless. When you intervene, reserve this potent weapon for extreme cases of causing harm for selfish ends. Interact with kindness when you can.

Contempt hurts. Whether hidden or overt, contempt hurts. We are social beings who care about the approval of people around us. Contempt from anyone erodes our sense of worthiness. Contempt from the people we physically and emotionally depend on feels like a threat to our survival. No one should have to endure an atmosphere of contempt.

In particular, children never deserve contempt. Some people aim corrosive contempt at children for their age-appropriate smallness and weakness. Those children swallow the idea that weakness is bad and go on to treat themselves and others with contempt, since we all have weaknesses.

Culture of contempt. As we become aware of how we and the people around us use contempt, we can minimize its presence in our lives. Where we find a culture of contempt, we can work to replace it with a culture of kindness and care.

Did you experience a culture of contempt in your family, community, or school? What qualities were held in contempt? Who was treated with contempt? Was contempt used as a way of signaling who was included and who was excluded? Was contempt discussed directly, or was it an acid drip in the background?

Inner contempt. If an inner voice treats us with contempt,

6: Relationship Skills

that part is usually worried that we will be seen as contemptible by the outside world. It is trying its best to help us survive with the tools it has. We can spend time with it and warmly listen for what it is worried about and what it wants for us instead. This part is often far younger and more terrified than it seems at first.

A young part that receives and collapses under contempt also needs to be heard with compassion. Spending time with these parts can give them the kind adult company they so desperately need, and help them shift toward kindness themselves.

Listening kindly to a contemptuous part is an inside job for the person containing that part, perhaps with professional help. You are not responsible for tolerating contempt from a friend or partner, even if you want to rescue them from their self-contempt, or you want to learn how to handle contempt better.

External contempt. Do you sense that someone in your life treats you with contempt? It might be as obvious as rolled eyes and silent treatment, or as subtle as a remark that stings and stays with you even though you are not sure why. We have sensitive detectors for contempt as part of our social survival skills.

People have contempt for someone they abuse, bully, or manipulate in order to distance themselves from their victim's inherent dignity and worth. Contempt is a symptom and a red flag, not a justification for abusing someone.

The way to handle external contempt aimed at you is to get away from it. You do not become immune by ignoring it. You cannot become good enough or work hard enough to deserve respectful treatment from someone who regards you as inferior, because you already deserve respectful treatment.

Contempt is emotional abuse and a relationship killer.

Limitations deserve care. As you find more compassion for yourself, you will also find more compassion for others. We tend to project inner contempt onto the people around us. We often have the most contempt for something we recently learned not to do.

When you notice contemptuous thoughts about others, silently acknowledge them. In what areas do you think of yourself as superior and others as inferior? If you were taught that, for example, people with intellectual disabilities are inferior, seek out information to counter that belief. Disabilities and limitations deserve care, not contempt.

Signals a problem. Contempt can also be a strong signal about a situation that needs your attention. When you feel contempt for someone's egregious behavior, pause to consider your options. You could distance yourself or ignore the problem, or you could take action to interrupt or change the behavior. If an individual is behaving badly, you could draw their attention to the problem and/or reach out to others for help. For larger social problems such as voter suppression or climate change denial, you could join an organization that is already taking action.

Culture of kindness. A culture of kindness is created by people who know how to be kind and considerate. Seek them out and learn from them. Notice how your body responds to being treated like a person who is already good enough. Pay attention to how they talk about and treat others, and practice those skills.

Where did you see a culture of kindness growing up? Were children allowed to be appropriately capable for their age and lovingly corrected for mistakes? Did you hear, "People do their best with the resources they have?" Did you celebrate people's successes rather than dwell on their failures? Was anger expressed openly with care, rather than leaking out as contempt?

Kindness includes empathic acceptance and clear boundaries, warm appreciation and respectful disagreement. Kindness is authentic, rather than being nice from behind a mask. In this time of isolation, simply acknowledging someone with kind eyes is a gift.

Struggle together. We are under tremendous strain from the pandemic, political upheaval, and increasing natural disasters. Contempt causes us to hide our struggles. The more we can be kind to ourselves and each other, the more we can struggle together rather than struggling alone.

Seek Nourishing Feedback

While feedback can often be thoughtless or contemptuous, it is most useful when it is careful and kind.

You want someone to take a look at an important letter before you send it out. Your kid left their shoes in the middle of the floor, again. Your boss makes little disparaging remarks about your Black coworker that she does not make about others.

We give and receive feedback constantly as we navigate our complex interconnecting social relationships. Some environments favor bluntness, while others favor more subtle signals. In environments where everyone agrees on the unspoken rules for feedback, communication proceeds fairly smoothly.

Feedback can be a mechanism for teaching, learning, and getting along better. It can also be a mechanism for status, control, and emotional abuse.

Affected by power. Feedback is heavily affected by power and privilege. People with more power tend to give casual direct critical feedback to those with less power. Feedback given to those with more power tends to be more indirect, subtle, and carefully thought out.

Positive feedback needed. We thrive on positive feedback, with the occasional bit of corrective negative feedback thrown in. Ideally, babies and young children are flooded with positive feedback from people expressing delight in their existence. This forms the foundation for a sense of being essentially okay that generates an internal flow of positive messages.

We do many things well, every day. We struggle with challenging circumstances and work within our limits as best we can. We make other people's lives better in small and large ways. We attend to our healing, and decline to pass on harm that was done to us. We do our best to show up and live well in a complex, heartbreaking world.

We deserve positive feedback for our efforts. We deserve to hear, internally and externally, "Well done. I see how hard you're trying. I see you are doing your absolute best." We deserve specific acknowledgement for things that go well, even maintenance tasks we do often, like cooking or laundry. We deserve praise for persevering in our private daily struggles.

Instead, most of us get a constant stream of negative feedback from our Inner Critic, who details every imagined and actual thing we do wrong. Even if we do many things well, we can always be criticized for something else we "should" have been doing.

Choose what to let in. While we are told that we "should" have positive self-esteem independent of everyone else, we naturally take in social feedback to check if we are good enough. Despite being hungry for reassuring positive feedback, we tune our senses toward the slightest sign that we made a misstep or offended someone.

Over time, we gain a clearer sense of our strengths and weaknesses. We know which of our qualities and behaviors people object to. We know which we are working to change, and which we have accepted as part of the package of being ourselves. We learn which kinds of feedback send us into a spiral of self-hate because they touch on qualities and behaviors we can neither change nor accept (yet).

We can choose which feedback we allow to touch us inside, and which we quickly discard with, "I can't go there," or "I can't emotionally afford that today." We can prefer to spend more time with people who are generally positive toward us, and at the same time will tell us kindly and directly when there is an issue to discuss.

We can find middle ground between using privilege to shield ourselves from uncomfortable feedback, and exposing ourselves to ongoing toxicity. When we already understand that we have a weakness, flaw, or problem, it does not help to hear it criticized repeatedly. Seek environments that recognize and reinforce tiny steps toward improvement. Just as we can prefer narratives with hope, we can prefer feedback that nourishes and supports us.

Acknowledge negative feedback. When we receive negative feedback that is new to us, we often respond defensively. Our Inner Critic may join in, reinforcing the negative feedback and criticizing our defensiveness. We can acknowledge the feedback and the speaker's feelings, and then take some time away from the conversation to process our reactions.

Most feedback has at least a kernel of truth. At the same time, people are talking about themselves most of the time. When we assume we are essentially okay, we can take in useful parts of feedback while leaving shame and blame behind. Acknowledging the feedback may be the only action we need to take, or we might need to change our behavior to stop doing harm.

Give clear feedback. When we give feedback, we can take some time beforehand to seek clarity on which parts belong to us, and which parts need to be said to the other person. What is the goal in giving feedback?

- **State a boundary or need.** People generally respond better to positive statements ("more of this") than negative statements ("less of that"). Both are valid.
- **Inform or teach.** Does the recipient want to be taught? Do they already know what you want to teach? Sometimes a brief reminder works well, such as "Shoes!" to the kid who left them out.
- **Reinforce hierarchy.** Think twice before giving negative or explanatory feedback to someone with less power.
- **Be heard.** The recipient may or may not hear you. At least, you get to hear yourself saying it.
- **Appreciate.** Give lots of (genuine) appreciation! It lifts spirits, fosters connection, and supports healing.
- **Acknowledge.** "You were right," supports people's sense of their truth and competence. Give this gift at every opportunity.

Delicate situations. Sometimes, remaining silent feels like colluding with an unacceptable situation, such as a manager disproportionately disparaging Black employees. At the same time, giving feedback feels useless, dangerous, or extremely delicate. There might be indirect ways of giving feedback, such as talking about microaggressions and implicit bias in general, or telling a story where the speaker realizes they were unfairly disparaging a certain group themselves. It might be possible to publicly or privately support the disparaged employees.

A gentle direct statement such as, "I feel uncomfortable when you talk down [specific employee] more than others," might contribute to change in the long run. There is no one way to give feedback in delicate situations. Remaining silent or waiting for an opportunity to speak are also valid options.

Feedback during bodywork. In my practice, I encourage clients to give me feedback about what they want more of and less of. It is part of the healing process to notice preferences, express them, and have them honored. Too often, we withhold feedback while receiving care because experience tells us that some practitioners do not want to adjust what they are doing based on client needs.

Entitled to kind feedback. We have a healthy entitlement to nourishing, supportive, kind feedback. We can also take care to give nourishing feedback to others. When we give or receive challenging feedback, we can do our best to skillfully speak and hear the parts that help us grow and change.

6: Relationship Skills

Careful Conflict

Expressing feedback can lead to conflict. Children growing up in abusive families not only associate conflict with violence and abandonment, but also miss out on learning about healthy conflict.

Resolving friction. Healthy conflict is about resolving friction between different people's needs and preferences. People in healthy conflict share goals to resolve a problem or repair a ruptured relationship. They may be angry and upset, but do not wish each other harm. In contrast, people in unhealthy conflict treat each other like enemies, with goals to win while someone else loses, take something from someone, or hurt someone. People with less power in an unhealthy conflict might be trying to escape without getting hurt.

Unconscious narratives. Our internal narratives strongly affect how we behave. We might hold unconscious narratives about conflict like, "I'm in danger," or "I'll get hurt," or "The best defense is a good offense," or "I always get what I want," or "I'm too nice to get into conflicts."

Notice how you fill in the story when you imagine someone saying, "I need to have a serious talk with you." What does the speaker look like? What size are they relative to you? What responses do you notice in your body? How do you expect the conversation to develop? How much room do you expect your voice to have?

Childhood experiences. When childhood conflict meant getting attacked, shamed, or erased, our bodies interpret any conflict as a threatening emergency and go directly into fight, flight, or freeze. Someone who feels strong and powerful might default to attacking with fists or words. Others might default to running away, avoiding the other person in the conflict, changing the subject, or dissociating. Still others might freeze or collapse, surrendering immediately to what the other person wants and apologizing for existing.

When we grow up being bullied or abandoned, it makes sense to walk on eggshells to make sure everyone is kept soothed and comfortable. We know in our bones that any conflict will be taken out on us. In contrast, when there are shared goals to meet everyone's needs in a respectful way, it makes sense to bring up issues sooner rather than later so they can be resolved together.

Reenactments. While there are plenty of conflicts in the present, some conflicts are reenactments out of the past, where we hold such a strong narrative that we pull people into acting it out with us. If the old narrative comes from only one person, then it can be resolved by owning it and becoming more aware of the present, perhaps by noticing what is the same and different about the past and present situations. The other person can step aside, declining to play their assigned role.

If two people's reenactments hook into each other, it can lead to a long, frustrating struggle to reach resolution. Even if one or both people recognize it as a recurring pattern, it can be difficult to disentangle a mutual reenactment.

For example, if Anat expects everyone to be critical, they might hear neutral statements as criticism and respond defensively. If Danika is not hooked in, she can simply say, "I didn't mean any criticism," and disengage. If Danika has her own narrative about being too critical or being misunderstood, the conflict might escalate rapidly, to both people's distress.

Listen and speak with care. A lot of conflicts arise because one person is not hearing another. It might be a momentary lapse, or a function of power and privilege, or an inability to see others' points of view. People with disabilities, and people who are marginalized in other ways, encounter conflict simply by advocating for room to live in the world.

No matter what the source of the conflict, it helps to listen and speak with care.

New patterns. If you respond to conflict with rage, panic, or collapse, first give yourself some empathy. Your responses make sense in the context of your experiences. Over time, take steps to calm your nervous system, both in general and specifically in response to conflict.

Observe the people around you and how they respond to conflict. Seek out people who want to resolve issues with kindness. Practice with tiny conflicts and gather new experiences that let you know the world does not end when you speak up. Reach out for support in handling larger conflicts. Let people know you are practicing new patterns.

Orient to the present, noticing differences from past conflicts. Tune into your senses. Feel your adult size, strength, and resources that let you engage in conflict as a respectful and respected equal.

If you feel small and overwhelmed in the middle of a conflict, ask for a break. When you are triggered, you will not have your adult skills available to find a positive resolution.

Listen with kindness to your own viewpoint. What outcome do you want? Is there an underlying issue? What are you afraid will happen? Is there a way to resolve this issue on your own?

Keep in mind that the other person's viewpoint makes sense to them. Listen to them with interest. Make room for them to be themselves.

For example, Danika is often late to meet Anat. Anat might choose meeting places where they enjoy spending time alone, recognizing that Danika is not good with time. Or, there might be an underlying issue around priorities and consideration that the two of them need to address together.

If possible, allow the other person to save face, as long as the problem is fully addressed for the future. Most people carry a lot of shame, and are reactive when they are feeling ashamed.

Avoid abuse. When you approach a conflict with kindness and positive expectations, that could bring the other person with you into healthy conflict or collaboration. Sometimes they are unable or unwilling to make the shift and will remain silent, avoid the conflict, or behave like an enemy. Whether they choose to cooperate or not, their behavior is not your fault.

If someone behaves abusively, you can name the behavior and tell them how you prefer to be treated. "No name-calling. Let's focus on behaviors, not personalities." You can also attempt to refocus on the issue at hand. If they continue to behave abusively, you can take a break and try again later. If you are not free to disengage, this is bullying or abuse rather than conflict.

Interdependence. The more we depend on others and they depend on us, the more we need ways to work out conflicts respectfully. We all deserve people in our lives who are kind even when they feel ashamed, angry, or upset. We should not need to keep people soothed to be treated well. Learning to manage conflict with care is a lifetime project for each of us.

Grow Away from Enmeshment

If there is never any conflict in a relationship, that might be a sign of enmeshment.

In an emotionally enmeshed relationship, there are two people, but only one point of view. All kinds of relationships can be enmeshed: parent and child, siblings, a romantic couple, close friends, coworkers, etc. Enmeshment is different from interdependence, where two people support and care about each other, but still maintain separate selves.

Usually there is a power imbalance where one person has the dominant point of view, and the other person merges with them. The dominant person might manipulate or coerce the other person, or the other person might initiate merging because that is their understanding of closeness.

Resisted separation. Infants start out emotionally merged with their carers. Ideally, the growing child has a secure base from which to gradually explore their separateness. The carer remains available to them for reassurance, and celebrates their developing independence.

When a carer signals disappointment in response to a child's explorations and encouragement in response to merging, the child will naturally tend to stay merged and suppress impulses to separate.

The signals might be unspoken and implicit: sadness and disapproval for separations, delight and approval for staying merged. Or they might be direct and explicit: "I need you close. Stay safe by me." The encouragement to remain merged might be mixed with genuine love and care, even as it thwarts the child's natural urge to establish their own point of view.

Signs of enmeshment. An enmeshed relationship has a sense of airlessness. You might feel yourself getting smaller over time, with fewer choices of behaviors and emotions. For example, you might always have to be the strong one who takes care of things, or alternatively you might always have to be the weak and fragile one. In a balanced relationship, your role shifts with time and circumstances.

You might feel overwhelming emotions that do not respond to your usual internal tools. One way to tell that an emotion belongs to someone else is that you cannot change or explain it. You can only acknowledge it, realize it is not yours, and let it go.

No quick fix. When you find yourself in an enmeshed relationship, there are many reasons to stay. You might want to walk away, and at the same time it feels like you and the other person are part of each other. Whether you are demanding enmeshment or acquiescing to it, you cannot simply turn it off.

You might leave the relationship quickly for safety, or end it gradually, or stay in it. No matter what happens with the relationship, you can grow into your own point of view over time.

Solid in yourself. The goal in healing from enmeshment is to repair your boundaries and sense of self. Rather than feeling woven together with someone else, you will gradually feel more solid in yourself, separate from others.

Because enmeshment touches into core attachment issues, you might experience intense shame as you explore how you relate to others and yourself. Be as gentle with yourself as you can.

Find your edges. To help you find your edges, you can practice a specialized version of the same/difference exercise. Name a couple of things that are the same between you and the other person, and a couple of things that are different. You might find one side much more difficult than the other. Keep practicing both.

You can also practice same/difference with point of view. Name a couple of things from your point of view, and a couple of things from the other person's point of view. Again, you might find one side much more difficult than the other. Keep practicing both.

Privileged points of view. Society reinforces some points of view and ignores or suppresses others. The more privilege you have, the more accustomed you are to thinking that your point of view is normal, correct, and the only way to look at things. The more marginalized you are, the more accustomed you are to thinking that your point of view is alternative, flawed, and unique to you.

Focus on yourself. If you have trouble finding your point of view, frequently take a few moments to pay attention to your thoughts, emotions, desires, and sensations. The first thing you might notice is guilt or shame for paying attention to yourself. Let those feelings know that you hear them, and continue to pay attention.

You are entitled to your own point of view, whether it is the same or different from other points of view around you. When you pay some attention to yourself, you are correcting an imbalance where most of your attention was turned away from yourself.

Focus on others. If you have trouble finding the other person's point of view, frequently take a few moments to listen for any information you receive about other people's points of view. If you notice a voice inside judging or invalidating other points of view, let it know you hear it and return to neutral listening. You are correcting an imbalance where most of your attention was turned inward toward yourself.

Boundaries. Your boundaries separate what is you from what is not-you. As you pay attention to your point of view as separate from others, your boundaries will naturally grow clearer. You will be able to both step forward to assert your point of view, and step back to make room for others.

You may get resistance from people who are used to being enmeshed with you, even when you assert your boundaries in small steps.

Enmeshment often includes Drama Triangle roles of Victim, Rescuer, and Perpetrator. From inside a Drama Triangle, anyone trying to exit looks like a Perpetrator, because they are changing the rules of the game. You have to be willing to be seen as bad and wrong to grow away from enmeshment.

Look for people who encourage you to stand in your story and celebrate your boundaries. Savor all the bits of support you receive for your growing separate self.

Internal points of view. We can also become merged with internal parts and try to speak for them, rather than listening for their point of view.

I often ask clients to listen to a body part in distress. "What does that sore hand have to say?" The client pauses to listen, and then says, "I'm telling it everything is okay now." Or they might say, "It wants to feel better," meaning, "I want it to feel better."

I ask again, "What does it have to say from its point of view?"

The client pauses to listen again. "It says it's angry." Now we are learning new information about what is happening inside the hand. I respond, "You might let it know you hear that." Acknowledgement is a powerful healing tool.

Balanced sense of self. Whether or not we are in an enmeshed relationship at the moment, we can benefit from clearer boundaries and more attentiveness to our own and others' points of view. Through a lot of trial and error, we learn to relate with respect both inside and outside ourselves. Growing a healthy, balanced sense of self is an ongoing process rather than a task to be completed.

The Right Distance from Family

Most parents have the deep instinct to protect small vulnerable beings, especially their own children. Some parents do not. Some parents are too overwhelmed, unskilled, or caught up in their own point of view to notice when they are causing pain in someone else. Some parents enjoy causing pain.

Many people say we "should" remain connected to our parents no matter how much harm they caused, no matter how enmeshed we realize we are, no matter how destructive it is to interact with them in the present.

Individual costs. It is true that there is a high cost to disconnecting from our family of origin and living without that foundation of support. Many people find it hard to imagine that in some families the foundation of support was never there in the first place. The cost of remaining in contact can be higher than the cost of disconnection, even though disconnection can include profound loneliness.

Siblings from the same family can have completely different perspectives on the costs and benefits of remaining connected. One child might emerge relatively unscathed, while another child receives the brunt of overt abuse and becomes the family scapegoat. Because that child shows symptoms and names the problem, they are accused of causing or being the problem.

Often a person who works on healing from abuse appears "crazy" and broken, while other siblings continue to navigate family relationships as if nothing is wrong.

6: Relationship Skills

Individual strategies. A survivor might choose different strategies for dealing with abusive parents at different stages in their life. When first remembering abuse, they might feel too fragile and too angry to interact with their parents at all. Or, they might love and need their parents alongside the abuse and remain in contact, perhaps in a more limited way.

Later, they might have more skills and resources to navigate the challenges of relating to abusive parents. Perhaps there are family members they enjoy, and it is easier to see everyone together. Or, they might want more distance than before.

Some abusive parents turn out to be wonderful grandparents, and might behave better to ensure they get to see their grandchildren. Or, some survivors fiercely protect their children from exposure to grandparents who continue to be toxic or dangerous.

Change for the better. Perhaps the parents have openly acknowledged past abuse, apologized, and made amends as best they can. (Heartbreakingly, this is not the way to bet.) Even if they are still abusive, perhaps setting firm boundaries keeps them in check enough to forge a workable relationship.

Sometimes one person's healing work is enough to shift a relationship into a better balance. Note: If a relationship does not improve, it means the healing person is not the source of the problems, not that they are not trying hard enough.

Too dangerous. Sometimes abusive parents remain too dangerous for contact. They might continue to commit physical or sexual assault on an adult child.

Often they are still emotionally dangerous. If there is no acknowledgement of abuse, there is a powerful gaslighting effect when everyone acts as if nothing happened. It can also be triggering to visit a childhood home. A survivor can be catapulted into feeling as trapped and helpless as they felt as a child.

Difficult to leave. Even if the relationship is still damaging, some survivors are forced to remain in contact through financial ties or emotional enmeshment. Like other abusive relationships, there are complex reasons to stay, and leaving can be a long process. Whether it leads to eventual lack of contact or not, clarifying boundaries both internally and externally can help over time.

Inherited trauma. In his book *It Didn't Start With You*, Mark Wolynn explores the idea that trauma is transmitted across generations, not just directly via unskilled or damaging parenting, but indirectly with mysteriously matching symptoms popping up unexpectedly.*

He also explores parental bonds that are fractured by early childhood trauma or separations, even though the parents meant well. In that case, it can be deeply healing to reconnect with parents as an adult.

We can walk away from abuse. We can work on healing and acquiring the skills we missed growing up. We can do our best to create chosen families. We cannot erase our roots. Those are still the people who bore or adopted us, the family we came from, the details of how home tastes and smells and sounds and looks imprinted deep in our bodies.

Whether it is possible for us to reconnect with our parents or not, it is useful to turn toward our roots and explore what trauma we might have inherited. We can explore our heritage of resilience as well, taking note of the survival skills we inherited.

---

* *It Didn't Start With You*, Penguin Random House, 2017, by Mark Wolynn.

6: Relationship Skills

Look for connections. Mark Wolynn suggests writing about a core issue or fear for a few minutes, allowing the words to flow onto the page. Take a break, and then read it over lightly, looking for phrases that seem especially charged or larger than the original issue.

For example, Sandy, the child of Holocaust survivors, carried an intense fear of closed spaces. Her writing included, "I can't breathe. I can't get out. I'm going to die." She was carrying the terror of relatives who were murdered in gas chambers.

The historical connection might be clear, as in Sandy's case, or it might take some family research to turn up a connection. If more family information is not available, we can "make up" a story to work with. We often know more than we realize, so the story can contain seeds of truth.

When we find or imagine a connection with a relative's story, we can contact that relative in our imagination and kindly return their story to them and ask for their blessing. We can also simply return what is not ours to the earth.

Parents in context. We can use a similar process to see our parents in context. What traumas might they have inherited from past generations? What got in the way of their ability to parent with warm attunement?

What age are they in your memories of them? Perhaps you are older than that now and can see them as struggling young adults. Do you know of events around that time that might have affected how they treated you?

Seeing parents with compassion is not meant to erase childhood pain or justify their behavior. When we step back to look at childhood abuse in a wider context, we see that even though we were personally hurt, it was not about who we were or how we behaved. No one deserves abuse.

Are there emotions or stories that you carry that belong to your parents? Imagine returning them to the earth and moving forward unburdened.

Held lovingly. Whether we connect with our parents every day, once a year, or not at all, we can reduce the internal charge we carry toward them. When we understand that abuse was not about who we are, we can release deep shame about not being seen and accepted. As we explore the history of our family, we can see ourselves held lovingly by past generations who wish us to be well and happy.

Support a Friend in Crisis

When we lack reliable connections with our family of origin, we turn to friends or chosen family in times of crisis.

Many of us, especially if raised female, are socialized to feel valuable by helping others. We might leap in to rescue a friend in distress, without regard to our own limits. We might get enmeshed in a helper role, always seeing the other person as someone who needs help.

At the same time, we might not know the best ways to be helpful. We might charge forward in Emergency Mode rather than taking time to assess what everyone really needs, including ourselves. Even in emergencies, pausing to assess lets us take more effective action.

The transition into a crisis is often abrupt. A sudden change or loss leaves someone grieving. A medical condition is diagnosed, or a scheduled surgery takes place. Even with a gradually worsening chronic illness, there is often a turning point where help is needed more than before.

While Susan Silk's Ring Theory* reminds us not to look for support from the person in crisis, we still get to have our own responses to the situation, including grief, anger, and disorientation. We might need some breathing room to process the shock of sudden change. We can seek support from people outside the crisis.

---

* "How not to say the wrong thing" by Susan Silk and Barry Goldman, April 7, 2013. https://articles.latimes.com/2013/apr/07/opinion/la-oe-0407-silk-ring-theory-20130407

Listen. When a friend is in distress, our goal is to listen for what they need and do our best to provide it, within our limits. We do not suddenly have to become a nurse, doctor, psychologist, parent, or mind reader.

The most precious gift we can offer someone in crisis is empathy and safe listening space for them to be exactly how they are right now. Let them talk or be silent. Let them cry or rage or be calm. Breathe with them. Listen.

When a friend is grieving, you could say:
- I am so sorry for your loss.
- I'm sorry you're hurting.
- I don't know what to say, and I'm here to listen.
- How can I help?
- I'd like to [practical offer] at [specific time]. Does that work for you? What would be better?

Do not tell them how to feel or try to fix them. Grief is not a problem to fix. Let their experience have the spotlight, rather than launching into your own stories. Do not make religious statements such as, "Your loved one is with God now," or "We never get more than we can handle." Leave that to their chosen religious leader.

Practical care. People in crisis, whether emotional or physical, often appreciate a specific offer of practical help. Be ready to modify it if they need something different. Practical offers might include laundry, house cleaning, bringing food, going for a walk together, or simply keeping them company for a while. Remember to check in with yourself about whether you have the inner resources to provide what you are offering.

Medical crisis. Recovering from surgery, Covid-19, or other medical crises can be scary and disorienting. The body hurts in unfamiliar ways and needs more help to get around than usual. The body might be busy detoxing anesthesia and metabolizing pain meds, which affect digestion, cognition, and sense of time and place. Feeling helpless and in pain is not only upsetting in the present, but can remind people of terrible times in the past.

Stay present. You can help your friend orient to the present by reminding them gently that it makes sense that they are confused and in pain. They get to feel however they feel. You might say, "You're having a hard time right now." Your calm companionship will help them find their way back to the present.

To stay more present:
- Take a deep breath, feel your breathing
- Drink some water
- Stamp your feet
- Name what you see around you out loud
- Hold a rock
- Say today's date and time
- (Add your favorite method here)

Support their strength. Support your friend's autonomy and adulthood. Ask them what they need, and trust them to know. Relate to them as an equal who temporarily needs help. Ask before touching them. Give them time to sense inside and reconnect with their preferences and boundaries after the invasiveness of surgery or other medical interventions. Support them in saying no as well as yes.
- "Would you like [X] right now?"
- "May I touch you to [do X]?"
- "Let me know when you're ready."

Self-awareness. It can be difficult to witness a friend's helplessness and pain. Your reactions and emotions can get in the way of being calm and supportive. Stay aware of your responses and tender places. Set your reactions aside for later when you can, and take a break if you feel overwhelmed. Stay present with your internal narratives about what it means to be helpless and in pain, and allow what is happening in the room make a new narrative.

Pain and helplessness can trigger shame in both of you, which makes everything harder. Acknowledge the shame and let it be in the room with you. Be mindful of the vulnerability of receiving help.

The transition out of a crisis tends to be more gradual than the transition into it. Little by little, the grieving person starts to feel better, or the patient's health improves. With an ongoing health condition, there might be a transition from short-term interventions to long-term care.

For some people, receiving help is uncomfortable and they exit the central role as soon as possible. Some people, through habit or privilege, relax into the central role and need to be nudged to start thinking about others' needs again.

Stay aware of your inner reactions to your caring role. If you notice persistent resentment, irritation, or overwhelm, you might need to step back even if your friend continues to need care or is not ready to relinquish their role. Eventually the give and take in your friendship needs to be rebalanced, or it becomes a caretaking relationship instead.

Already enough. Remember that you are enough, just as you are. Your friend is enough, just as they are. Bring kindness and respect for everyone, including yourself, when you are supporting a friend through a crisis. Our relationships with strangers, friends, and family are crucial to making it through difficult times.

Resources

Taking the War Out of Our Words, Voices of Integrity, 2016, by Sharon Ellison offers non-defensive questions, statements, and predictions to navigate conflicts.

How to Talk So Kids Will Listen & Listen So Kids Will Talk, Simon & Schuster Trade, 2012, by Adele Faber and Elaine Mazlish offers respectful communication skills with anyone, not just kids.

Running on Empty, Morgan James Publishing, 2012, by Jonice Webb, PhD describes the effects of emotionally neglectful parenting, including lack of affirmation.

Recovering from Emotionally Immature Parents, Echo Point Books & Media, 2019, by Lindsay Gibson has good information on how to establish better relationships with emotionally immature parents as an adult, if the parents are not dangerous to be around.

Victory Over Verbal Abuse, Adams Media Corporation, 2011, by Patricia Evans describes how to heal from the aftereffects of verbal abuse, which includes contempt.

It Didn't Start With You, Penguin Random House, 2017, by Mark Wolynn explores inherited trauma and tools for releasing it.

Embodying Hope

7: Healing Support

Healing starts exactly where we are and unfolds from there, no matter how much we wish we were somewhere or someone else. Healing is about how we perceive and relate to the world as well as ourselves.

We do not leave trauma behind. We grow around and through it, integrating it into our self and body as we engage with our life as it is right now.

In difficult times we need support for what we are going through in the present in addition to ongoing healing for past trauma. Over time, we discern what kind of help works best for us, and what gets in our way or causes more harm. Our bodies know what we need to find relief, ease, and self-trust.

We practice relationship skills with our practitioners, including boundaries and graceful endings. We embody hope every time we reach out for support, holding our past hurts and disappointments with tenderness.

Celebrate Small Steps

Acute trauma forces sudden, overwhelming, drastic change on the body. It is natural to expect that some equally drastic treatment can undo the change and restore health. Chronic trauma can be an accumulation of sudden blows, or a long-term lack of essential nurturing and care.

Unlike trauma, healing is slow, gentle, and incremental. Healing from chronic trauma might include learning new skills that were missing in childhood, which is also a slow process. We learn to relate to ourselves more kindly, even though the effects of trauma are not erased.

Pause for relief. One of my jobs as a practitioner is to hold a sense of progress for my clients, both within a session and over the time we work together. Within a session, we pause together to notice a shoulder that is more relaxed, a deep breath of relief, or the "cheering section" of belly gurgles. We take note of a more hopeful thought about an issue, or a new idea that floats up.

In our daily lives, each of us can take time to soak up relief, hope, and ease when they arise. Our bodies like to spend more time at ease. We naturally do more of what feels good, so we reinforce positive patterns when we give our attention to enjoyment.

Acknowledge successes. Over the long term, a client's nervous system settles more quickly during a session, and they bring in stories of successes that would not have been possible in the past. Our work together gradually shifts as old issues are resolved and new issues come to the fore. We all tend to forget about what stops bothering us or what we completed, turning our focus toward new goals just out of reach. How does it feel in your body to pause and acknowledge a recent success or shift?

Some clients deflect positive words. They might fear being set up for ridicule if they dare own their success, or feel that "boasting" is not allowed, or worry that something bad will happen if they let down their guard. They might want to ensure that their negative feelings are not erased. Those responses make sense after coming through difficult experiences.

Uneven progress. Healing from trauma has its ups and downs. When a client falls in an emotional hole, it can be an opportunity to notice how much they have improved overall. "Remember when you used to feel like this all the time?" It can also be a chance to notice how much more quickly they return to balance than they did in the past.

One clear sign of progress in healing from trauma is decoupling present triggers from past strong reactions. For example, at first a client might respond with frozen terror when the sheet touches their neck. Later in their healing, they might be able to say, "I don't like that," and move the sheet away. It is still an uncomfortable sensation, but does not kindle an overwhelming nervous system reaction.

Slow change. While we might occasionally notice a big shift, most change happens one small tentative step at a time. We might need to experience a new possibility many times before it overrides an existing pattern. Bodies prefer to have time to adapt to change.

We can also celebrate small actions we take in the direction of healing, or any large goal. As a gift to your future self, take a tiny step forward now, so that the next tiny step will be possible tomorrow. Valuing only larger steps can block progress entirely.

Allow stuckness. Progress and improvement are wonderful to see, and at the same time, clients do not have to improve for the practitioner's benefit. Some clients find it helpful or supportive to continue to come in even when we do not see a lot of change. Sometimes bodies rest for a while to gather strength for the next change. Sometimes depression or stuckness lasts a long time. We do not have to improve to deserve care through hard times.

Chronic illness and disability can be opportunities to notice a different kind of progress. Perhaps we are better able to honor our limits or find helpful care. With defeat, failure, or downturns, perhaps we can be more gentle and less self-critical than in the past. Perhaps we can go through a recurring pattern with awareness, even if we cannot yet change it.

Practice feeling better. One of the main goals of healing is to feel better. We can work directly on that goal by bringing our attention to anything that feels better, and staying with the pleasant feelings for as long as feels right to us. Celebrate each small improvement. You deserve recognition for the hard work and learning and letting go that made it possible.

Solid Support for Change

A lot of narratives about healing focus on change rather than on feeling better. We take on goals to change how we handle the past and the present, change our circumstances, identify what is broken and fix it. Many of us believe that we are fundamentally not good enough, and if we yell at ourselves a lot, we might eventually change to become good enough. It feels terrible to be yelled at all the time, and we never seem to improve enough to make it stop.

Already deserve support. Instead, we can decide that we are already good enough, and there is always room to learn from our mistakes and keep growing. Healing can include learning new skills and letting old survival tools fade into the background. At the same time, a lot of healing is about adding resources and support rather than tearing down what is already here. We do not need to be fixed.

We do not need to change first to deserve support. We need and deserve support no matter what. It can be hard to find practitioners who offer refuge rather than fixing, especially when something inside insists on being fixed.

Place to stand. We need a place to stand to make any kind of change, a stable foundation to risk the unknown. As we feel safer and more secure, we become curious about exploring small changes, and then larger ones. Pushing ourselves to change is counterproductive. If we had everything we needed to make a change, we would be making it. We naturally hold more tightly to what we already have when we feel unsafe or threatened.

For example, when I lift a client's arm during a bodywork session, they often reflexively stiffen and hold their arm up. If they apologetically tell their arm to relax, I tell them it is my job to offer their arm enough support to feel comfortable.

When I shift my hold, or let their arm rest on the table, or communicate my intentions more clearly, their arm may relax. Sometimes it has a deeper reason to stay tense, and that is okay too. The goal is to connect with how the arm is feeling right now, not to demand a change.

Energy to adapt. Change is inherently disruptive. Even if the change takes us toward what we want, it requires time and energy to adapt.

When we are coping with unexpected change, it can feel like the rug has been pulled out from under us and we need to find ground under our feet. We can find support by reaching out to friends for reassurance, taking time to breathe, and noticing what is still the same in the midst of change. We can inventory the inner resources and external support we already have.

Listen to resistance. When we consider initiating a change ourselves, there is often a part that wants the change, and a part that emphatically does not. Rather than trying to power through resistance, we can pause and listen.

Listen with understanding and empathy for all parts. Slow down, and acknowledge each bit of information you receive. It might come as words, or images, or sensations, or a vague something that slowly becomes more clear. If you find yourself listening with frustration, impatience, or an agenda, that is also a part that needs to be heard.

Unwanted and wanted. Sense for what, specifically, the resisting part does not want. What, specifically, is bad about that? Often this part is trying to protect you, and appreciates being heard in detail about its efforts.

Also listen to the part that does want the change. Sense for what, specifically, this part wants. What, specifically, is good about that? What does this part want you to experience in your body? Can it show you that experience right now?*

After listening to both parts, the change may feel less urgent, or more clear. The parts may find they want the same things underneath their struggle. If the struggle continues, keep listening.

Others' reactions. As we reach out for support around change, we might notice subtle (or not so subtle) signals from the people around us that say, "Don't change. Stay just the way you are." Our current patterns might fit neatly with theirs, like matching puzzle pieces. If we change shape, we might not fit with them anymore. The more closely enmeshed we are with someone, the harder it is to change in our own direction.

We might look around after an internal shift and wonder why we feel at odds with friends and communities that used to feel harmonious. Change has costs. As we heal and become more centered in ourselves, we may lose some relationships we valued, and need time to grieve.

Freedom to experiment. There is a turning point in healing from trauma, from learning new skills to learning to embrace exactly the way we are in the world. As we feel more solid in ourselves, we feel more freedom and flexibility to experiment and change. When we have more inner and outer resources, it is easier to take risks and try something new.

---

* Phrasing suggested by Ann Weiser Cornell and Barbara McGavin as part of Untangling®.

Add Ease to Anniversaries

Healing means being able to keep ourselves company through the effects of a trauma or loss, rather than erasing them. An anniversary might bring more abundant flashbacks and other PTSD symptoms, or a resurgence of grief.

We might want to dismiss a difficult anniversary as no longer relevant, but the body insistently brings it to our attention. Even when we are not aware of the exact date, bodies track the time of year through the angle of light, smells in the air, type of clothes we wear, and other sensory input.

Is this old? We wonder why we are so off-balance, and then realize it is the day of the car crash, or the assault, or the death of a dear friend. Or maybe we know that a certain time period is hard for us and dread it coming around every year.

When we acknowledge our feelings and ask, "Is this old?" we can get a welcome sliver of distance. Old feelings can be intense and absorbing, and at the same time we know that they will pass. Since they are from the past, there is nothing we need to do to fix them. We can let them wash over us like a wave, and come up for air in the present. We can also reach out for support, letting others know about the anniversary.

Remind yourself, "These feelings are old. They will pass." You can set feelings aside in the room when they get too big.

Separate causes. The first step to improve a difficult anniversary is to notice that it is not the time of year itself that brings distress, but our associations with it. That separation makes room for change. We can work with the distress directly, and also build more positive present-time associations with the time of year.

Add enjoyment. For example, if autumn is a difficult time, you can acknowledge the painful feelings, and also notice what you enjoy about the season. There might be colorful trees around you, or you might enjoy the feeling of wearing long sleeves, or you might like the foods that come into season in autumn. Even if nothing enjoyable comes to mind at first, bringing your attention to the present mixes some light and air with old pain.

Witness self. Paying attention to the present also helps us connect with our larger witness self, who can make room for old feelings without being overwhelmed by them. Bring your attention to your senses. What are you seeing, hearing, tasting, smelling, touching right now? What chair, floor, or other surface is supporting your weight? How is your breath moving your body?

An ongoing meditation practice can help strengthen your witness self. A meditation practice can be as simple as: pause for a few minutes and notice whatever happens during that time, including resistance to noticing.

Anniversaries can bring up split-off parts that hold emotional intensity from a traumatic event. We can invite those parts closer during the rest of the year so they can integrate and heal rather than being frozen in time.

Same/different. An anniversary can bring up thoughts that everything is the same. "I can't believe I'm still in this place!" or "I can't believe I'm in this place again." Or, an anniversary of a loss can bring up thoughts that everything is different, "I'll never have that again."

Usually our brains prefer one or the other. Either we want everything to be the same so that we can lump it all together and manage it the same way, or we want everything to be different so we can manage each one individually and not become overwhelmed. Paying attention to both can help anchor us in the present.

Practice both sides. When a troubling anniversary comes around, list a few things that are the same as last year, and a few things that are different. If your brain prefers sameness and struggles with difference, you could note that you are a year older, with another year of experiences to bring to this anniversary. You might have learned new skills or made new friends. If nothing else, the weather is probably different than it was on this day last year. Even if the pattern feels exactly the same, moving through it with awareness is already a change.

If your brain prefers differences and struggles with sameness, you could recall a memory of how things were last year, and note that you can still feel how you felt then. The capacity for that feeling is inside you and cannot be taken away. Perhaps you sit at the same desk, or visit the same places, or see the same people.

Birthdays and holidays. Birthdays can be an annual trigger for many people. They are supposed to be happy occasions, so it can be even more painful to remember being abused during a birthday. Some parents cannot let their child be the center of attention even on that special day, so they are cruel and demeaning to make the child feel small.

Birthdays can be a reminder of inexorable aging. They can also be a marker of what we "should" have accomplished by a certain age, even though everyone's circumstances and resources and path through life are different.

Similarly, holidays can also bring up painful memories of lost good times, or painful contrast between loneliness and the cozy family experience we are "supposed" to have. Take some time to sit with what you want for your holiday or birthday, as well as noticing what is the same and different from other years.

The pandemic has interrupted default celebrations everywhere, forcing us to stop and think creatively about what aspects are important and how to make some part of that happen safely at a distance.

Disentangle kindly. Our brains are wired to see patterns and associate memories with times of year. Each time we move through the cycle of the seasons, memories come up to be acknowledged and healed. When we can be a kind witness for our hurting selves, we can disentangle painful feelings from the time of year that brings them up, bringing more ease in the present and laying the foundation for more peace in the future.

Elements of Refuge

When anniversaries or other triggers become overwhelming, we can seek out professional support.

Unresolved trauma acts like an internal abrasive, leaving a survivor's nervous system feeling raw. After trauma ruptures both emotional and physical boundaries, we feel exposed and endangered. Each change in the environment has to be evaluated as a possible threat.

Practitioners can provide a calm refuge for overwhelmed survivors by offering a stable container around logistics, emotions, and the healing relationship.

Sturdy frame. A practitioner creates a sturdy frame around sessions with careful attention to consistent details. Sessions that start and end on time are reassuringly predictable and trustworthy. Some clients like having the same time slot every week, while others appreciate flexibility that gives them access to care when their schedules vary.

A physical space that stays the same becomes familiar and comforting. All the elements of a stable frame help clients orient to the present and separate it from the past. "I recognize this room. I feel safe here. That traumatic event is not happening now."

When a practitioner does not provide a stable frame, traumatized clients will struggle to make progress, while more resilient clients will be able to take instability in stride. This makes it easy for the practitioner to blame traumatized clients as "resistant to treatment" rather than addressing the problem in their practice.

Gradual transitions. Transitions are hard for everyone. They are especially hard for traumatized people who already feel off balance in an unreliable world. Transitions into and out of a session need to be similar each time and give the client time to adjust. External stability and consistency make it safer to explore internal change.

Hold space. A sturdy emotional container is equally important. The practitioner gives the client plenty of room to experience big emotions, while staying right there to offer accompaniment, help with regulation, and teach tools to manage emotions.

Non-judgmental kindness, warmth, and acceptance create safe space to acknowledge internal truths and explore painful wounds. A gentle, respectful approach allows the client's defenses to soften and Inner Guardians to go off duty.

The practitioner holds space for clients by staying present with them, while silently acknowledging and setting aside their own emotions and reactions. At the same time, it can be healing for a client to hear a practitioner's authentic responses such as, "Wow, I feel angry when I hear how you were treated." It is important to respond to a client's story in a caring way while keeping the focus on them.

Strong boundaries. The client/practitioner relationship also needs steadiness and protection. Of course, the practitioner maintains confidentiality for everything that happens in the session, and respects the client's boundaries. The practitioner also honors their own boundaries around fees, appointment times, and being treated with respect. This brings their presence more solidly into the room and models good boundaries for the client.

Dual relationships. The practitioner stays mindful of their healing role, and avoids dual relationships (additional roles) with the client. A dual relationship might be an additional business relationship (for example buying something from a client), friendship, or sexual relationship. Sexual relationships with clients are ethically forbidden. Other additional roles need to be carefully considered, always with the well-being of the client in mind.

Dual relationships make the therapeutic container more fragile. Discord in an additional role (for example the item purchased from a client is faulty) carries over into the therapeutic relationship. The roles of practitioner and client are inherently uneven, which conflicts with a more equal friendship. The client might feel pressured to take care of the practitioner in sessions, or the practitioner might feel pressured to continue to be "on duty" in the friendship.

Dual relationships also threaten the confidentiality of sessions. Information or events inside a session might "leak" into conversations outside the session.

Clear roles. Dual relationships work best when they are temporary, include a lot of open communication about the risks, and meet a need for the client. For example, a survivor might not feel comfortable receiving bodywork from a stranger, so they prefer to go to a friend. In small communities and rural areas, it might not be possible for a practitioner to maintain a strict separation from clients.

Both practitioners and clients can make dual relationships work better by carefully separating the different roles. During a session, the focus is fully on the client, and personal matters are set aside. At other times, sessions are not discussed and the practitioner is not expected to hold space.

Survivors of childhood abuse experienced damaging lack of clarity in relationships where their parents were also abusers, and perhaps also required the child to take on parental roles, all veiled in secrecy. It can be both unfamiliar and relieving to have clear roles when receiving help.

Internal container. Over time, survivors internalize safe containment they experience with practitioners. Survivors can intentionally create a vivid image of an internal container to use when their practitioner is not available. When traumatic memories and emotions become overwhelming, visualize placing the traumatic material inside the container to be held securely for a few hours or days until there is time to process it, either alone or with help. While the material cannot be put aside indefinitely, it is useful to have more choice about when to process it.

Relief and ease. Survivors long for a protected space for healing, and practitioners long to help them. When practitioners pay careful attention to the elements that create a refuge, it removes distractions from the healing process and brings relief and ease. Gradually, survivors regain, or gain for the first time, a sense of safety and reliability in the world.

When Help Means Danger

Survivors have to learn how to navigate both internal and external barriers on the way to finding professional support.

Neglect and abuse cause invisible losses: skills and experiences that simply did not happen. For example, a bodily sense of safety from being tended and held with gentle hands. A deep sense of deserving care from having physical and emotional needs consistently met. The confident knowledge that there are larger, stronger, wiser people by your side who will do their best to protect you.

Internal barriers. The first internal barrier is realizing that help is needed. Kids tend to assume that their home life is normal. A survivor struggling with depression and anxiety might assume that everyone has similar struggles, or that they are defective or broken.

Another internal barrier is lack of awareness that effective help exists. Psychotherapy and psychiatry might appear threatening and alien, part of a different world. The stigma of a diagnosis might outweigh the possibility of receiving help. When a survivor does not know anyone who goes to yoga or acupuncture or bodywork, it is hard to imagine receiving help there. Abusive families might imply or say outright that practitioners are adversaries.

External barriers. A survivor who decides to seek help quickly encounters external barriers, needs for:

- Money and/or insurance to pay for care
- Nearby kind, skilled, trauma-informed practitioners

with space in their practices
- Transportation
- Time and energy to get to appointments and do emotional processing between appointments.

Physical disabilities and marginalized identities make getting help even more complicated. Perhaps the office needs to be wheelchair accessible, or fragrance-free. Practitioners can offer better care if they understand the implications when a client is bisexual, or has immigrant parents, or is a person of color. Finding a cultural match in a practitioner can bring relief in itself.

Telehealth or online appointments can solve some of these issues, and add new needs for a device, a good internet connection, and privacy at home.

Good fit for now. Searching for practitioners is a skill that a survivor might not have learned growing up if they did not see their parents seeking help. It can feel overwhelming to step into the unknown world of finding and sorting through practitioners for a good fit.

At the beginning of the healing process, the survivor is probably in Emergency Mode and needs to learn the basics of managing triggers and overwhelming emotions. They can benefit from a lot of approaches, since everything is new to them.

Years into their healing process, survivors have learned the basics that most trauma-aware practitioners offer, and it will be harder to find a good match. Some survivors find a long-term practitioner who can help throughout their healing process. Others find pieces of what they need in different places and learn to look for a good fit for now, rather than a good fit forever.

Initial appointments. Navigating initial appointments is a skill in itself. Some practitioners want a full trauma history up front, which can be re-traumatizing. Some survivors feel ashamed of pent-up emotions that spill over in a first conversation, while other survivors warily avoid self-disclosure. It makes sense to be a mix of scared, off-balance, and guarded when getting to know a new practitioner.

Pain around needs. For survivors whose parents reacted with disgust when they expressed needs or shamed them when they asked for help, developing a trusting relationship with a practitioner is a healing process in itself. They might find it excruciatingly hard to ask for anything or say that something makes them uncomfortable.

When a parent is both abusive and nurturing, a child is left with both deep longing for safe nurturing, and bodily terror in response to nurturing closeness.

For the adult survivor, there is a small window of tolerance for receiving help. The sessions have to be beneficial enough to keep returning, but gentle and slow enough to avoid triggering terror of being invaded.

This can lead to awkward sessions at first to figure out what works and establish enough trust to continue. It helps if the practitioner and survivor can be on the same side through that initial struggle, sharing the goal of discovering and meeting the survivor's needs.

Reenactment. Sometimes the practitioner and survivor join in a reenactment of old dynamics. For example, the survivor has a recurring pattern of being given too much advice, and the practitioner notices a repeated tendency to give them advice. Ideally the practitioner will notice and name the reenactment. Over time, survivors will recognize repeated patterns and can bring them up to address together.

Practitioner issues. Many survivors are exquisitely sensitive to hidden power struggles and victim blaming. Some practitioners are invested in seeing survivors as small, helpless, and broken, rather than as strong, capable people who need some help.

Some practitioners label it "resistance" when a survivor does not respond the way they expect, rather than helping a survivor connect with and trust their own internal process.

The practitioner might get triggered into their own issues. Over time, survivors begin to recognize when that happens and are able to say, "That isn't mine." If it happens occasionally, it can be an opportunity for repair. If it happens too often or is not repaired, then it is not a good fit.

The practitioner's worldview might be threatened by what happened to the survivor. The survivor ends up protecting the practitioner from their story, which does not contribute to their healing. For example, the practitioner might want to believe, "Women can't be abusers," or, "Mothers always care about the well-being of their children."

Boundary practice. Interacting with a practitioner is inherently practice with boundaries. How much to let them in, how much to keep them out. How much to ask for. When to say "No" to a treatment, technique, or exercise to protect an irritated nervous system, and when to risk opening to the unknown. How much to bring in our whole selves, both the parts we are proud of and the parts we are ashamed of. How much to smooth things over and how much to allow conflict to arise.

When to stay, when to leave. All along the way, a survivor holds the difficult balance between the benefits of treatment and the costs in time and energy and money. How long to wait to see positive results. How much of a mismatch to tolerate before seeking a different practitioner, or going without treatment for a while.

Knowing when to stay and when to leave is a skill many survivors simply do not have at first. We may stay in harmful situations, or leave quickly when a repair might have been possible. Over time, we gather more knowledge about internal signals, and about what sorts of care are available. We learn to make sincere attempts to repair a problem, and then give ourselves permission to walk away if the situation does not improve.

Sometimes there will be no right answer to a dilemma. We can widen our focus to include our ongoing healing process and say that any answer is okay. We are still okay no matter what we choose. There comes a point when working harder at healing is not the answer. We need to take a break from telling ourselves we are not good enough.

Relational injuries. When the first people to care for us also hurt us, when our injuries are relational, of course it will be difficult to manage relationships with practitioners. We can soften the difficulty when we can keep ourselves company through the process, witnessing our struggles with compassion.

7: Healing Support

When Help Means Rescue

While survivors of childhood abuse are often wary of receiving help, we also long for rescue.

Dreams of rescue. Children growing up in abusive or neglectful homes dream of their "real" parents sweeping in and scooping them up, or running away and finding a better home somewhere else, or being careful and quiet and good enough not to be abused anymore, or finally making someone understand the hurt and horror so they would step in and make it stop.

Children build their dreams out of the stories they absorb from books, shows, movies, games, online content, and the people around them. They project themselves onto the main characters of stories, and think, "When I am like that, my life will be better." They gather a conscious narrative about what rescue looks like, as well as implicit assumptions and expectations about it.

Beliefs about help. Depending on what we experienced in childhood, we might believe that helpers require us to be small and helpless to make them feel strong and powerful. We might believe that we need to keep a careful eye on the helper's needs, because they must be kept happy before they will help us. We might believe that helpers require payment through emotional enmeshment or sexual favors.

Children reach toward whatever warmth is available, like a plant in rocky ground reaching for light and nourishment. Adult survivors also reach toward warmth and help, but with more "shoulds". We "should" be able to distinguish between true help and manipulation. We "should" be able to take in help even if it is overwhelming or triggering. We "should" get better in a certain time frame. We "should" be able to let it go, put the past aside, rise above our history, forgive our abusers, and above all not make any trouble for the people around us.

Growth, not a journey. When healing is seen as a journey, helpers are seen as more powerful rescuers who take us away from a bad place and move us to a better one. When healing is seen as growth starting from where we are, helpers remove obstacles and add nourishment and support. They help us become more ourselves, rather than transforming us into someone else.

When we believe in the narrative of being broken and needing fixing, we look for people who want to fix us. When we shift to a narrative of being essentially okay, and needing to learn new skills and find support, we look for people who want to support us.

Validation and responsiveness. Above all, survivors need validation and support for believing our truth. Most abuse includes gaslighting. "You're imagining things." "There's nothing to be upset about." "You're crazy." Helpers who want to fix survivors often reinforce that narrative by telling us what is wrong with us, rather than what is right in us.

Survivors also need responsiveness and attunement. A primary injury in abuse and neglect is not being heard when we signal pain and distress. We need helpers who show us moment by moment with their attentiveness and care that our well-being does matter in the world. When mis-attunement is not swiftly repaired, it reinjures survivors in a tender place.

New ideas. At the same time, help includes presenting new ideas that might feel dangerous at first. When a helper says, "You are allowed to have needs," the survivor might feel a flood of suppressed needs for kindness and care, as well as a panicked Inner Guardian who says, "Absolutely not! Needs are unsafe, weak, bad, wrong."

When a helper has clear boundaries and steps back from being enmeshed, a survivor might feel rejected and abandoned, pushed away from the only kind of care that is familiar.

Strong emotions. When a survivor tentatively starts to feel safe with a helper, strong emotions can arise. Long-suppressed anger might come up about past lack of safety, and about feeling vulnerable. Anger can be welcomed and allowed to move through. Safety includes space for all emotions.

Feelings of safety and positive attachment might be entangled with sexual attraction. Practitioners are ethically bound to hold clear non-sexual boundaries. Practitioners who allow or invite sexual contact add another layer of abuse and confusion to the survivor's burden. Sexual feelings can be allowed to move through without acting on them. Any shame that arises with and around them can also be kindly and gently allowed to move through.

Telling secrets. Telling old secrets about abuse can evoke intense feelings of both terror and bonding. There might be younger parts urgently wanting to tell and get help, while urgently wanting to stay silent and safe. All the parts need to be heard and respected in the process of sharing about past abuse. Telling can be an important part of healing, and at the same time it is not required at any point.

Choose a goal. Healing might not look anything like what we expect. It might be more gradual, less terrifying. More lonely, less merged. It might not change parts of us that we want to leave behind. It might change core assumptions that we never thought to question.

How can we evaluate whether practitioners are good for us with so many intense emotions and longings around help and rescue? It helps to choose a concrete goal, discuss it directly with the practitioner, and evaluate over a few sessions whether there is any progress toward the goal.

The goal might be emotional support during a crisis, improvement in a specific symptom such as nightmares or anxiety or physical pain, a life change such as getting out of a relationship or finding a new job, or learning new skills to better manage triggers and activation. We can also notice whether there are unexpected improvements in other areas, or an unexpected increase in symptoms.

Monitor how it feels before and after sessions. Simply feeling better after sessions is a good reason to continue seeing a practitioner. If your gut tightens beforehand and you feel worse afterward, those are signals to strongly consider changing practitioners, or at least discuss the problem directly. Feeling unable to bring up issues with a practitioner is also a strong signal.

Shift goals. It might be possible to see progress in a single area with a practitioner, even if they are not helpful generally. Kristin H. sent me this great example of evaluating a new therapist.*

> *"After four hours with him and his style that felt 20 years old and completely unhelpful for where I was in the journey, I asked him if we could just do a half session*

---

* Private communication, October 3, 2018, quoted with permission.

to strategize about a particular area he seemed to have a lot of knowledge in. Afterwards, I thanked him and asked if I could just contact him in the future if I got stuck in that specific area."

Self-rescue. Even if someone comes along and plucks us out of an abusive environment, we still have to do the internal work of healing. In the end, we each have to reluctantly, angrily, step by step, rescue ourselves.

At the same time, we receive kindness, help, and support from people around us even when they are not in a formal helping role. A well-timed piece of advice, a tip about a job opening, a warm smile from a stranger, a friend's consistent emotional support. When we look back, there were little bits of rescue along the way, even if a single dramatic rescue never happened.

How to Leave Your Practitioner

Leaving a long-term practitioner is also a skill, one we do not get a chance to practice much and probably did not learn growing up. We might learn the polite, "I don't think this is a good fit," while we decline to reschedule with someone we saw once or twice, but it is harder to know how to end with someone we have seen for a long time.

Even with short-term practitioners, we have to learn to trust our instincts about when to ask for what we need, and when to back away from the bog of not being understood.

When we finally connect with a practitioner who does understand, who is giving us some of what we need, we relax into the refuge of their help. We naturally become attached to their care. Over months and years we grow and change, and so do they. One day, we notice we are feeling uncomfortable and restless. Or perhaps receiving help has felt dangerous all along, and we reach a tipping point where we need to address it.

Pause to notice. We might wait a while to see if the rough patch resolves itself. We might sit with what changed inside us and in them and see if we have a request for what might meet our needs better. We might notice that our priorities have changed around how we spend our energy, time, or money. We might realize that we are clearly done, or even if it is not clear, that we want to try something different for a while.

We might feel like the practitioner is in a position of

authority, and we need their permission to leave. We might feel surprised, confused, or guilty that their work does not fit anymore. We might feel angry about ways our needs are not being met now. We might worry about hurting the practitioner's feelings or making them angry. We might worry about how to find someone who can better meet our current needs.

Choices. We could try a smaller change first, like shorter or less frequent sessions. We can also look for a new practitioner before stopping with the old one. Nervous systems often appreciate a more gradual transition.

We might urgently want to leave right now, and that is always our right. We are under no obligation to continue seeing any practitioner. We can check inside whether the urgency comes from a present-time event, or a past-time trigger. Note that triggered responses, "resistance," feeling stuck, and unexplained discomfort are all valid reasons to stop.

We can choose how much or how little to communicate with the practitioner about wanting to leave. Speaking openly about how we feel might lead to a new phase of productive treatment, or respectful acknowledgment of our need to leave. Either way, it is an opportunity to make conscious choices about how we end a relationship that has been positive.

Practitioners are people. While we might feel some responsibility to take care of the practitioner's feelings, we do not have to protect them from our truth. We can practice using "I" statements and naming what is going on for us, hopefully with their encouragement and support. They are there to help, and unless they are just starting out, they have faced this situation before. They know clients grow and change and leave over time.

If the practitioner is not respectful of the decision to leave or becomes defensive when receiving feedback, we can retreat to the polite and disappointed, "This is no longer a good fit."

At the same time, there is no need to burn bridges by being intentionally hurtful or attacking. Even if we are angry with a practitioner, it is our responsibility to cancel any upcoming appointments rather than simply not show up. Best to tie up loose ends and not be left liable for an unpaid session. Practitioners are people and deserve basic respect for their time.

Sample sentences to use with practitioners, preferably during a session, or by email, text, or phone between sessions:
- "Can we talk about what completing treatment and stopping would look like?"
- "I'm feeling uncomfortable with our work lately." Possibly add specific reasons or, "I'm not sure why, but the feeling isn't going away."
- "I've noticed that my symptoms haven't changed much." Possibly add, "I'd like to focus on improving [specific symptom]."
- "I've realized that I need [specific need]. Is that something you can provide or recommend someone for?"
- "I've appreciated our work together, and it's become clear to me that I need some time off. I'll let you know when I'm ready to reschedule."
- "I'm feeling a lot better, so I'm thinking of tapering off our sessions."
- "I'm leaving town (starting school, changing jobs, etc.), so my last session will be on [date]."

Smooth the way. Practitioners can smooth the way by checking in with clients if they seem less engaged with their sessions, or if there is a plateau in their progress. By opening a conversation about ending, they show that it is a safe topic for discussion. Clients might also need reassurance that they are welcome to continue even without obvious progress.

Closure. The practitioner may offer a final session for closure. A formal ending could be healing, in contrast with sudden, jagged endings that often come with trauma. A final session can include appreciation from both sides, acknowledgement of any unresolved conflicts, and discussion of next steps. A practitioner can celebrate the client's changes and achievements in their time together.

If the ending is sudden because the practitioner died unexpectedly or the pandemic caused them to close their practice, that can be traumatic in itself. Let yourself grieve the loss of that supportive relationship, and find closure over time.

Congratulations. Choosing to leaving a longtime practitioner is like graduation. You have learned and grown and healed, and it is time to face new adventures. It might feel scary, and at the same time it is cause for pride as you look at how far you have come. It might also bring grief for a safe space and healing connection that you are outgrowing.

In difficult times, it can be harder than ever to find support. You might discover unsuspected inner resources and strengths as you move forward on your own. Take some time to celebrate all the ways you are embodying hope by making it this far.

Resources

The Educated Heart, Lippincott-Raven Publishers, 2005, by Nina McIntosh gives great advice for bodywork practitioners, with concrete examples.

"Finding the Line" by Nan Narboe is a clear introduction to why and how practitioners should create a secure frame. http://nannarboe.com/FindingTheLine.html

Choosing Gentleness, Compassionate Ink, 2018, by Robyn Posin offers warm encouragement and support.

Through the Shadowlands, Rodale Books, 2017, by Julie Rehmeyer chronicles her descent into Chronic Fatigue Syndrome and ultimate ascent into carefully managed recovery with good support.

Afterword: Thank You

Thanks to each of you for pausing for a moment, putting down your struggle, taking a breath, and hearing that you are okay just as you are right now.

Thanks to each of you who leaves behind the numbing blanket of denial to explore your individual history of abuse and trauma. Thank you for stepping away from the consensus of the crowd to stand shakily in your own island of truth. Thank you for being willing to feel alone there, and know that many of us cheer you on from our own truth islands. Thank you for breathing through terror.

Thanks to each of you who finds steadiness in knowing and understanding and being certain, and is also grimly patient with uncertainty and not knowing and bewilderment. Thank you for trudging through transitions one moment at a time, allowing yourself to live into your new shape and skills and environment as slowly or as quickly as the process needs to happen.

Thanks to each of you who is in conversation with shame, discerning past shame from present, yours from other people's. Even though shame may silence you or double you over in pain at times, thank you for being willing to be vulnerable and visible in the humble grandeur of your authentic self.

Thanks to each of you who is harnessing anger, letting it flow without flooding you, choosing words and actions with care rather than spraying anger at everyone around you. Thank you for letting anger support your boundaries and fuel your resistance.

Thanks to each of you for defiantly finding joy, for expanding into your full self and savoring delight wherever you find it. Thank you for connecting warmly and loving with fierce protectiveness.

Thanks to each of you who wields power collaboratively, mindful of everyone who is affected. Thank you for finding the middle way of compassion, neither avoiding power nor becoming lost in it. For being open to the aches of the world, for including other points of view, thank you.

Thanks to each of you who is doing the work of acknowledging privilege and dismantling racism and white supremacy. Thank you for taking the next step in front of you: reading, learning, listening, speaking, supporting, leading. Thank you for doing activist work privately, publicly, and politically.

Thanks to each of you who is wearing a mask during the pandemic, despite the awkwardness and discomfort and fogged glasses. Thank you for protecting the people around you as well as yourself. Thank you for taking action to reduce the spread of Covid-19 and shorten the pandemic for all of

Afterword: Thank You

us. Thank you for specifically, concretely saving lives.

Thanks to each of you who is sitting with the pain of isolation, gritting your teeth, wailing aloud sometimes, remembering all the other times you have been isolated and wondering if you did all that healing for this? Thank you for building your capacity to tolerate discomfort and pain without rushing to relieve it. Thank you for having the strength to get through, even though I'm sorry you had to go through all the struggles that built your strength.

Thanks to each of you, raw with stress and grief, who knows that we are all raw and still manages to be kind. For nodding from the sidewalk, for putting a little extra warmth into transactions at the store, for making sure people around you have what they need, for mending what you can reach, thank you.

Thanks to each of you for working so hard to be a good person. You are succeeding, minute by minute. Yes, you, especially if you think that I could not possibly mean you. There is no endpoint, no "good person" badge to pin to your shirt or post online, just the ongoing effort. Thank you for caring for the world. Thank you for caring for yourself.

Thank you for embodying hope.

Embodying Hope

Glossary

Some glossary entries refer to previous books, *Wellspring of Compassion* (abbreviated *Wellspring*) and *Presence After Trauma* (abbreviated *Presence*). You can also find the articles online: https://TraumaHealed.com/articles/by-topic/

Ableism — Discrimination or prejudice against people with disabilities. Many common metaphors are ableist. For example, "blind" for unaware, "lame" for poorly executed, "crazy" for mean, bad, or unwise. See "Practice Kind Language" on page 19.

Acceptance — Making space for all aspects of our present experience, including the parts we hate and the parts we are ashamed of and the confused muddle we cannot even sort out into parts.

Activation — Tension and increased stress, "fight, flight, or freeze" response of the sympathetic nervous system. See also **Settling**. See "Find Calm: A Polyvagal Primer" on page 150.

Agency — The capacity to take action. See "Agency in a Time of Pandemic" on page 43.

Attachment — A loving bond between child and carer, or between two adults. Attachment can be secure or insecure. See "The Push/Pull of Touch" on page 140.

BIPOC — People who are Black, Indigenous, and/or People of Color. Pronounced "by-pock." See "Rock the Boat About Racism" on page 56.

Boundaries — A flexible container for sensations, emotions, and preferences, separating "me" from "not-me." See "Grow Away from Enmeshment" on page 193.

Bullying — Repeated, aggressive acts in the context of a power imbalance. See "Interrupt Bullying" on page 197 in *Presence*.

Cis, Cisgender — Someone whose gender identity matches their assigned gender at birth. Opposite of **transgender**. See "Prefer Narratives with Hope" on page 7.

Consent — An unforced moment-to-moment agreement to participate in a specific activity. See "Enjoy Enthusiastic Consent" on page 253 in *Presence*.

Decision-Free Zone — A safe time and space to listen to all of yourself, with a clear boundary that action is off the table. See "Decision-Free Zone" on page 19 in *Presence*.

Developmental trauma — Ongoing violation and/or abandonment by trusted people during childhood. See "Find Calm: Practice Rest and Regulation" on page 145.

Dissociation — Spaciness, disconnection, feeling distant from current experience.

Double bind — A situation where any choice leads to punishment, you can't leave, and you can't discuss the situation.

Glossary

See "Step Away from Double Binds" on page 85 in *Wellspring*.

Drama Triangle — Three interlocked roles of Victim, Rescuer, and Persecutor. People involved in the drama can fluidly shift roles, or all three roles can be internal to one person. See "Compassion for the Drama Triangle" on page 162 in *Wellspring*.

Embodiment — Being present with our full physical and emotional experience. See "Introduction: Here We Are" on page 1.

Emergency Mode — A state of urgency and panic that continues after a traumatic event even though safety has been restored. See "Exit Emergency Mode" on page 134 in *Presence*.

Emotional abuse — Words, body language, and other behaviors that bully someone into feeling defective.

Emotional labor — The detail work of caring, noticing, and paying attention. See "The Sacred Work of Showing Up" on page 257 in *Presence*.

Flashback — Intrusive sensations, emotions, and reactions from unprocessed traumatic events which impinge on a trauma survivor's present-day life. Flashbacks are a hallmark symptom of **PTSD**. See also **Trigger**. See "Flashbacks: Experience Distress in Safety" on page 111 in *Wellspring*.

Focusing — A simple method for connecting with yourself. When you notice a sensation or emotion, you can keep it company, listening for its truth without expecting it to change.

Freeze, frozen — Physical collapse, stillness, and dissociation from the body in response to an overwhelming threat with no possibility of overcoming it. See "Find Calm: A Polyvagal Primer" on page 150.

Gaslighting — Psychological abuse that attempts to destroy the victim's trust in their perceptions of reality. See "Repair Your Reality After Gaslighting" on page 172 in *Presence*.

Healthy entitlement — A flexible, balanced sense of our wants and needs in relationship to others. We are entitled to complete autonomy over the insides and surfaces of our bodies. See "Healthy Entitlement: Discern Your Domain" on page 122.

Hope — Continuing to take action in the face of not knowing. See "Introduction: Here We Are" on page 1.

Inner Critic — Internal voice that tells you everything you have done, are doing, and will do wrong. See "Good Enough for Mistakes" on page 27.

Inner Nurturer — Internal voice that knows you deserve care and respect and there is nothing wrong with you. See "Resonate with Loneliness" on page 99.

Larger witness self — See **Witness self.**

Meditation — Sit comfortably, take three slow breaths, and notice what happens. Okay, now do it again. There, you're meditating! See "Meditation: Safe Space for Noticing" on page 56 in *Wellspring*.

Microaggression — A reminder about white supremacy or other system of oppression, seemingly minor, but still hurtful, especially with repetition. See "Rock the Boat About Racism" on page 56.

Oppression — To crush or burden by abuse of power or authority. To unfairly treat some people as less than others. See "Rock the Boat About Racism" on page 56.

Glossary

Post-Traumatic Stress Disorder (PTSD) — A label for the nervous system's long-term response to trauma. Diagnostic symptoms include intrusive memories (**flashbacks**), avoidance and emotional numbing, and anxiety and increased emotional arousal.

Presence — Sensing one's experience right now.

Privilege — Rights, advantages, and immunities given to people for having certain characteristics, one or more of white, male, straight, cisgender, wealthy, Christian, able-bodied, etc. Privilege is the other side of **oppression**. See "Rock the Boat About Racism" on page 56.

Resilience — Ability to recover from shock or injury. Yielding and springing back into shape like a living tree branch. See "Agency in a Time of Pandemic" on page 43.

Resource — A source of support and strength. Resources can be external, such as a friend or a safe place, or internal, such as taking a deep breath to connect with the present moment. See "Withstand Ongoing Trauma" on page 39.

Same/different exercise — Name a couple of things that are the same, and a couple of things that are different. Can be used with triggering events, enmeshment, anniversaries, etc. See "Add Ease to Anniversaries" on page 216.

Settling — Relaxation and decreased stress, "rest and digest" response of the parasympathetic nervous system. See also **Activation**. See "Find Calm: A Polyvagal Primer" on page 150.

Somatic Experiencing® — Trauma healing techniques developed by Peter Levine. See "Heal Around the Edges" on page 10 in *Presence*.

Surrender — Submitting to a threat. Waiting for an

opportunity to resist. Letting go of internal resistance. See "Surrender Without Shame" on page 215 in *Presence*.

Tone argument — Silencing someone with less power or privilege by criticizing their tone instead of listening to their message. The tone is often judged for being "too angry." See "Deflect the Tone Argument" on page 193 in *Presence*.

Transgender — Someone whose gender identity does not match their assigned gender at birth, including people who are gender-fluid, genderqueer, or nonbinary. See "Prefer Narratives with Hope" on page 7.

Trauma — An event or ongoing situation which overwhelms a person's available coping skills and resources.

Trigger — An internal or external experience that stimulates a traumatic memory. Triggers can come through any of the senses, or through a thought or emotion. They can be subtle, such as the light at a certain time of year. See "Triggered! Now What?" on page 138 in *Presence*.

Victim-blaming — The belief that if victims had behaved differently, they would not be coping with bad news now, so it must be their fault. No one deserves abuse for any reason. See "Demand Respect, Not Victim-Blaming" on page 78 in *Wellspring*.

White supremacy — The pernicious, pervasive idea that white people are more important and deserving than everyone else. See "Rock the Boat About Racism" on page 56.

Witness self — The accompanying wholeness that can turn toward an inner emotion, memory, or experience with kindness and compassion. Also called larger witness self. See "Good Enough for Mistakes" on page 27.

About the Author

Sonia Connolly offers intuitive, compassionate bodywork in Portland, Oregon for sensitive people healing from trauma. Sessions are now available online.

She is a survivor of incest, emotional abuse, and ritual abuse, and has sensitivities to gluten and fragrances. She embodies hope through helping people heal, meditation, creativity, bicycling for transportation, gardening, petting her cat, and Balkan dancing and singing.

Learn more and sign up for free monthly healing articles at TraumaHealed.com.

Does this book spark a response in you? I'd love to hear about it! Send your thoughts to sonia@TraumaHealed.com.

Embodying Hope

Illustration Credits

All images licensed as Creative Commons unless otherwise specified.

Cover photo, Robert Bye, Desert Boulders, Ein Gedi, Israel. https://unsplash.com/photos/VkZuNpXxdIg

Section heading illustrations and article headers by Robyn Posin, used with her gracious permission.

Kidney figure 1999-2020, Rice University. https://openstax.org/books/anatomy-and-physiology/pages/25-3-gross-anatomy-of-the-kidney

Abdominal organs figure from Anatomy of the human abdomen by Ties van Brussel. https://en.wikipedia.org/wiki/Abdomen

Lungs figure from Henry Gray (1918) *Anatomy of the Human Body*. https://commons.wikimedia.org/wiki/File:Gray965.png

Respiratory system figure 1999-2020 Rice University. https://openstax.org/books/anatomy-and-physiology/pages/22-1-organs-and-structures-of-the-respiratory-system

Eye figure by Bruce Blaus. "Medical gallery of Blausen Medical 2014". WikiJournal of Medicine 1 (2). https://commons.wikimedia.org/wiki/File:Blausen_0389_EyeAnatomy_02.png

www.ingramcontent.com/pod-product-compliance
Lightning Source LLC
Chambersburg PA
CBHW031310150426
43191CB00005B/165